WHY JOHNNY DON'T KNOW JESUS

Mama, Don't Let Your Babies Grow up to be Apostates

PETER CHRISTIAN OLSEN

ST. LOUIS, MISSOURI

ISBN: 978-1-60350-067-8

Published by Lucas Park books
www.lucasparkbooks.com

Printed in the United States of America

Contents

INTRODUCTION

A not so imaginary conversation

Sherri and I sat down to have a conversation. I offered her a beer, but she refused it. Ever since she decided to go to theological school and become a youth pastor she has turn out to be a teetotaler.

"Let's talk," I began.

"Okay, I'm listening," she replied.

"There is good news and bad news. Which do you want to hear first?" I asked her.

"Give me the good news first", she responded with an air of misgiving. The tone of her voice implied that she suspected all the news to be bad.

"Okay" I said. "Here's the good news. Teenagers still have a genuine interest in religion, particularly Christianity. The majority still attends church, participates in youth groups, and goes on mission trips."

"Yeah," she replied. "Nothing new about that. So what's the bad news?"

"Well...," I hesitated for a moment. I didn't want to disappoint her all at once "Well, they do all this but have no understanding why."

"What do you mean, they don't understand why?"

"I mean they are just going through the motions, pretending to be Christian, but they haven't the slightest understanding of what the Christian faith is all about".

"But they participate in the church programs, and doing mission service is Christian busywork, isn't it?"

"No harm in that," I assured her, "but what appears to be the dominant religion among American teenagers, according to most research, is mostly about feeling good, being happy, and becoming successful in life. Their faith is a sham. God is nothing more nor nothing less than a therapist that the teens turn to for solving their immediate problems. There is a dichotomy at play here, teenagers increasingly claim to be religious, but their religion is anything but Christian."

End of conversation.

....

There is an old saying often attributed to Mark Twain: *"There are three kinds of lies: lies, damned lies, and statistics."* Recent statistics (and of course some polls) indicate a frightening trend. Adolescent attitudes toward Christian faith have undergone drastic changes. Teenagers have abandoned the traditional faith and replaced it with a watered-down simplistic apostasy that has little or no similarity to Christian faith. American teens remain clueless about traditional Christian faith; the depth of its meaning is beyond their comprehension.

But here is where the dichotomy occurs. Despite their dearth of knowledge, teens continue to participate in Christian communities in record numbers, and openly acknowledge the importance of faith in their lives. How is it possible for them to draw strength from a Christian faith about which they are ignorant?

Caught up in this dilemma of teenage apostasy is the age-old traditional Confirmation education. Teenagers receive more of their religious education at the time of confirmation than at any other time of their adolescence. Confirmation, that venerable religious ritual seeking to nurture adolescent faith has many supporters, yet is fraught with detractors. Supporters claim it as the foundation for strengthening adolescent faith. The critics claim it has lost its purpose. Both sides site data to support their arguments.

Recent polls give credence to the detractors. This is not just an indictment of confirmation, but also a rejection by adolescents of tradition religious beliefs in general. Perhaps rejection is a misnomer. They don't necessarily reject

Christian practices; they just don't know anything about them. They are ignorant of Christian beliefs. Some statistics from the Pew Research Center are revealing:

- Seventy percent of Protestants between the ages of 18-30 drop out of church before the age of 23.
- Six out of ten children (59 percent) believe that religion has a negative influence on the world.
- Nearly two-thirds of teenagers don't believe in God and think that reality television is far more important than religion.
- Surveys show that 66 percent of teens do NOT believe a deity exists while 59 percent have never prayed and 16 percent have never been to church.
- 60 percent of teens say they only go to church for weddings and christenings.
- Only 30 percent of teens think there is an afterlife while 10 percent believe in reincarnation.

Statistics may not always be exact and precise but they do indicate trends. While teenage participation in organized religion may hold steady, ignorance of basic tenets of Christian faith is becoming the norm. The value of Christianity for teens is waning drastically; it has lost its authentic theology and has become merely a set of principles for successful living. It leans less of theology and more on psychology. What the statistics do NOT reveal is why; why are teenage religious beliefs changing so drastically; why have they become so indecipherable; why are teens so ignorant of Christian faith and practices?

As a clergy person, I taught confirmation and worked at youth ministry for over twenty-five years, probably way past my ability level. I gave limited consideration to why I taught confirmation, what I expected, or how best to nurture faith in adolescents. I just plugged along, kept on keeping on, and repeating the traditional programs and structures. I never took the time to justify what I was doing. Only much later did I choose to scrutinize this phenomenon of adolescent faith initiatives. Better late than never.

During the past decade or two, much research has come to bear upon the religious practices of teenagers (notably *Soul Searching, The Religious and Spiritual Lives of American Teenagers*, by Christian Smith and Melinda Lundquist Denton, Oxford University Press, 2005). Social scientists and religious pollsters report a sorry state of American teenage attitudes toward Christian as well as other traditional faiths. This conclusion causes great angst among religious educators. Teenagers, they tell us, don't know Jesus; have minimal awareness of the basic tenets of the Christian faith, have distorted views of the biblical God, and portray a religion of "whatever," which is nothing more than a shrug of the shoulders at the thought of absolute truth.

The gist of this research relied on raising specific questions. Among them where the following:

- What do American teens think and believe about Christian faith?
- How do they practice this faith, if at all?
- What can be done to enrich their religious experience?

The result of the research exposes a tenuous nature of teenage religious beliefs or lack thereof. Left undone by the researchers, however, are potential remedies. Little is offered by way of solutions. No parent wants his or her child to grow up to be an apostate, least of all, not you or me. During this past decade, I choose to spend my energy, resources, and some extended effort seeking to discover the "mystery" of adolescent's faith and practices; why we are failing them, and how we might remedy this situation.

The framework of my concern is always in the context of confirmation education. Confirmation remains a foundation for nurturing adolescent faith formation. Because so many adolescents pass through this program, it's requisite that it be the locus for renewal. The content of this book addresses confirmation education as it is presently undertaken and argues that there is considerable room for improvement.

Section one of the book, more or less, presents the following format as a structure for sharing ideas, suggestions and conclusions. Section two (addendum) includes a variety of resources for practical consideration for the religious educator.

Section One

The way we have always done it: Protestant and other religious congregations have relied heavily on the "way we have always done it" as the primary planning tool for confirmation. When we look closely at these "ways" we find a whole host of assumptions passed on from generation to generation with minimal reflection. No consideration is given to the possibility of change, or even slight adjustments to accommodate new understandings about how adolescents learn. Curriculums lack content and some even detract from purpose. Knowing these assumptions enables the religious educator to differentiate between "what is," and "what might be."

The state of adolescent religion and faith practices: Almost every decade produces a whole host of researchers bent on examining the life styles of American teenagers. The year 2006 produced a ground breaking study that concluded that American teens are "ignorant" of the basic tenets of the Christian faith. In this section we examine the present state of adolescent faith and practice. Much information and detailed explanations are forthcoming that give credence to the conclusion that the religious faith of American teens is anything but healthy or authentic.

Christians under construction: Creative methods of instruction and/or teaching techniques can stimulate interest in subject matter normally boring or uninteresting to adolescents. The most creative methods rely upon teenagers' insatiable curiosity and imagination. While capturing biblical curiosity about the nature and mystery of God, teenagers are exposed to concepts of doubt and uncertainty, not as hindrances to faith formation but rather as resources toward clarification and amplification.

What's the purpose: We are a purposeful people. Everything we do is to accomplish a purpose. Unfortunately we are not always clear about the purpose of confirmation education. Purpose is intentional. The intent of confirmation is student centered; what we want to happen to the student, not what the teacher wants to teach. Clarification of precise purposes for confirmation greatly enhances the chances for successful faith formation.

Creedal thinking: As a way of stating beliefs and defending them, creeds serve to heighten conversational faith. Getting teenagers to talk about their beliefs is essential for faith formation. Conversation breeds understanding and insight. Creedal thinking is a process that allows teens to express beliefs and principals, both secular and sacred, that opens up dialogue. Dialogue heightens awareness.

Belonging: Communities are obligatory for human growth, even more so for the vulnerable adolescent. Only to the degree that each person in confirmation has a place "where everybody knows my name" will that person be open to trust, the foundation of faith in God. Trust begins with a sense of belonging and what constitutes belonging is the focus of this section.

Best practices: Faith formation: If you are to ask an adolescent what faith is, don't be surprised if the answer is something like, *"believing something that isn't true."* We have a responsibility to our students' minds, but we have a more profound duty to their souls to sensitize them. Our task as apostles to the young is to lead them, like God, to understand and express the self-not merely the "sometime spirit" that emerges by chance during a dutiful hour in worship, but the spirit that *is* the teenagers child's true self. But that will require a major conversion, in teachers and administrators, from our pervasively pragmatic and efficient mind-set. The concept of "practice" is the foundation of faith formation. We teach almost always from the perspective of faith *formation* rather than faith *information*.

What Works: For confirmation to be a source for faith formation we need to distinguish between spiritual curiosity and creeping apostasy. Faith formation is a crap shoot, that's the dilemma we face as religious educators. But we can learn from each other. Pastors and others are polled and reveal what works for confirmation education under a variety of circumstances.

Section Two.

Addendum: This concluding section presents a variety of work book activities. Confirmation is nothing if it is not "hands on". Each of these sessions employs a teaching method I have found meaningful and attention grabbing for teenagers. If and when they must put the "rubber to the road" and actually talk about and get involved in their own faith formation, the activities in this section provide that incentive.

I sincerely hope that even if the content does little to inform your educational venture, that it might, at the very least, start you on a spiritual journey.

1

"BUT WE'VE ALWAYS DONE IT THAT WAY"

An introduction to the practice of Christian confirmation

The atmosphere in the Church feels drenched with solemnity. Fourteen adolescents, dressed in white robes, line up across the front of the congregation. They are kneeling, facing the altar. There is a look of bewilderment on their faces. Directly behind them stand their parents and God parents. The pastor slowly walks down the line placing her hand on the head of each student. She then exclaims "Jonathan, I confirm you in the name of the Father, the Son, and the Holy Spirit. Amen." She walks to the next student. "Marilyn, I confirm you…" After she confirms all fourteen, the pastor's hand feels greasy.

Parents and God parents surround the confirmands. Each student's relatives place their hands upon individual heads while the pastor shares a communal prayer invoking God's blessing. The kids begin to squirm and reach up to straighten their hair. Each confirmand receives a white rose, a symbol of purity and innocence, but no one is quite sure why. At the conclusion of the service, all proceed to the church fellowship hall for a reception of punch and cookies. Each member of the congregation ushers by to congratulate the confirmands and welcome them into membership in the church. The members, however, are unaware that this may be the last time they will see these teenagers, at least in church.

A colleague of mine suggested to his Board of Christian Education that he would like to delay confirmation for a few years until the youth are a bit older and a bit more mature. He cited excellent reasons for doing so. Commitment to the church is a mature decision beyond the grasp of junior high students who are too young to comprehend biblical concepts and most importantly, he (the pastor) just didn't get along with junior high teens. He also cited statistics that indicated younger students are more likely to drop out after confirmation than those who are older. He proposed that in the future confirmation be a one year program for high school juniors or seniors.

The Board tabled the idea. They said they needed to cogitate on the matter for a bit. "Let's bring it up again at our next month's meeting, "they agreed.

Next meeting came and went. No mention of his proposal. Soon autumn approached, the time just prior to the beginning of a new confirmation class, the one the pastor wanted to postpone. No decision. Finally in late September, the Board responded to the proposal.

"We've given this serious consideration, "the Board president stated, "but don't think it's a wise idea."

"Why is that?" my friend inquired.

"Well we just think we need to keep the program as it is for our junior high age students, "they responded.

My friends pressed the issue. "But why do you think it's best for junior highers?"

Then came the coup de gras. "It's working the way it is. We've always done it this way. Leave it alone. We need to get on to others matters." That settled it.

Confirmation is a human concoction.

Confirmation is a religious tradition. It is as indigenous to the Christian religious landscape as Christmas, Easter, and Holy Matrimony. It has a long and glorious history, having its roots in the ancient Christian community.

Scriptural teachings do not mandate confirmation. It is a human fabrication. Evidence shows confirmation is modeled after an academic tradition embodied over centuries – a time of preparation, the teaching of fundamentals, catechism tests, and an elaborate graduation rite replete with robes and sometimes mortar board hats. It appears that the church copied this model to give legitimacy to the ceremony of confirmation and as a means to recognize young religion students for the spiritual plateau they achieved.

Confirmation was originally bestowed before baptism by the eastern branch of the church (Orthodox) and after baptism by the western branch (Catholic). Over the centuries, however, confirmation has come to signify a "completion" of baptism. In the American experience, where we like a bit of pomp and circumstance, confirmation has taken on a life of its own, almost sacramental, if not in fact, at least in attitude.

Although rejected by most denominations as a sacrament, confirmation remains as an important religious "coming of age" celebration. We recognize it as a catechetical experience closely tied to one's preparation for first communion and as a completion of one's baptism vows. Its status as a rite of initiation into church membership has become paramount, if not over-emphasized. Expectations are mixed. Once confirmation is completed, confirmands often assume this means release from further obligations and public commitments to the Christian faith. It is a graduation ceremony, an ending.

The congregation has a different perception. They see it as an official initiation into the Christian community; a beginning point towards further and more mature involvement in the practices of the faith and church. We make every effort to include the confirmand into the life of the congregation. Fear reigns supreme among many in local churches, however. When adolescents disappear right after confirmation, panic sets in. Church folk fear that might mean there will no longer be a next generation to carry on the ministry of the congregation.

Claiming confirmation success

What's the best confirmation program? No one knows for sure. All kinds and types of programs are tried. Some are quite adequate, meeting both religious and educational expectations, while many others are found less than sufficient. For some it's the "we've always done it this way" attitude that prevails. If confirmation was good enough for grandpa, then it's adequate for grandchild. Pastor planned and pastor led, the essentials of Christian theology and history and mission are dispensed ritualistically.

For others, innovations are necessary. A program filled with retreats, discussions, and relationship building is presumed far superior than the traditional pastor/lecture approach. Knowing about Christian faith and practices is less important than relating to other Christians.

Despite attempts at differing approaches, much of the tradition remains the same. The age of confirmation has endured, usually occurring somewhere between the 6th and 9th grade (ages 12-15). The leadership and teaching functions rightfully belong to the pastor. Congregations view the ritual less as an educational venture and more as an entrance into Church membership, a coming of age ceremony.

When we claim success with confirmation education programs, it is most likely a personal judgment using a subjective standard. Different religious traditions have different expectations. Discovering common criteria for "success" remains elusive and highly speculative, primarily due to the lack of objective criteria for evaluation. Those who have taken the research seriously do conclude there is some significance of confirmation as a tool for teaching basic Christian tenets.

Memories have much to do with evaluating confirmation education. Adults like to reminisce about their own experiences back in the 50's and 60's when confirmation might have been an all day Saturday session or a Sunday afternoon and evening. A catechism was learned by rote memory. Examination by deacons or elders was a common practice; a feared prerequisite for being confirmed. The confirmation program was a socializing experience for young people as much as an educational venture. Recalling the experience actually brings back fond memories despite that they faced confirmation with fear and trembling.

The attitudes of teenagers today are strikingly different. They anticipate the process with a certain ambivalence. School, clubs, and sports schedules minimize the need for confirmation to be a social experience. Any respect for the tradition comes as polite deference to older siblings and parents, but underneath there is trepidation and a great deal of anticipated boredom. I have often overheard remarks bordering on "stupid" and "dumb" by adolescents contemplating classes in confirmation education, but not in hearing distance of their parents. For the adolescent today, confirmation is just another obligation necessary for pleasing parental expectations. That's a strong motivation to participate.

Pastors, the traditional teachers of the confirmation program, complain that it has become a sterile ritual, outliving its usefulness in its present state, and in need of a major overhaul. One noted pastor, William Willimon stated in an article *Taking Confirmation Out of the Classroom* that he couldn't help recalling an Episcopal priest friend of his say, *"Confirmation is a second-rate junior high commencement ceremony after we have marched the kids through a series of boring classes and then laying-on-of-hands to graduate them out of the church."* (Christian Century, March 16, 1988, p271.used by permission),

Not much has changed over the last century. The confirmation program still involves the same age group, uses the same content, and employs the same teaching strategies with very little new innovations. It continues to be a staple for most Protestant congregations. Hardly a church exists, with the exception of nondenominational congregations, which does not promote confirmation and its ensuing preparation as a highlight of both the young person's spiritual experience and the congregations continuing tradition.

Religions habitually hang onto rites and rituals long after both their utility and function, and sometimes even the intended meanings, have long since disappeared (The world is flat, the sun revolves around the earth, and virgins should be sacrificed). One of the most cherished creeds of the church is, "But we've always done it that way." Traditions are strong motivators and a compelling force for continuity. The very first expectation laid upon me at my first pastorate fresh out of seminary was, "How soon can you get the confirmation class together? We always begin in October so the kids will be ready for the confirmation service at Pentecost?" When I hinted that I had no experience in teaching any subject, much less confirmation, and wasn't sure how to go about it, I then asked, "Are there some experienced teachers in the congregation I can call upon?" The Christian education committee looked aghast. "But the pastor has always taught the confirmation class," they exclaimed. "Besides, the Women's fellowship has already set the date and assured us they would serve refreshments after the confirmation service." So it goes, confirmation will happen one way or another whether the pastor likes it or not *"cause that's the way we've always done it."*

Common characteristics of confirmation education

Upon careful examination of confirmation education, both as "the way we've always done it," as well as a challenge to develop in teens "an unchanging faith in a changing world," there continues to exist some common characteristics. We discuss here some of these common traits as a means to help understand the present state of confirmation. Only by understanding what is, can we begin to examine what might be.

Confirmation is for adolescents: We can't say for sure because we have not visited with every available congregation in North America, but we are fairly confident that all congregations, including Baptists, have reasoned that twelve through fifteen is the ideal time for confirmation. It's not a bad time, but is it the ideal time?

We already are aware that adolescents, particularly younger ones, remain aloof to theological considerations. They just are not into religion. Religion is extraneous to their lives. Despite our labors, which may not be our best efforts, teenagers remain inarticulate and ignorant of basic Christian tenets and practices. Yet even knowing this we persist entrenched with the idea that adolescence is the best time for confirmation; the process of faith formation.

Is there demonstrated proof that spiritual formation happens best at thirteen? Probably not. It's better to assume that parents think that 13 year old adolescents are still at the age where they can be controlled, forced to attend assigned classes, and not yet ready to rebel. That makes for a better set of circumstances for the adults but not necessarily for the adolescents. Spiritual maturity and physical maturity do not dovetail.

Most research in education indicates that because spiritual awareness requires a high degree of abstract and conceptual thinking, the more mature the person the greater the possibility the person will absorb theological material. It takes a mature person to comprehend the language, the symbols, and the stories of spiritual expression. Adolescents are one step removed from the concrete stage of development where they think only in terms of what they see, hear, taste, and feel and yet we want to burden them with the abstract and often mysterious concepts of faith. This may prove to be beyond their intellectual ability at this age and stage of development.

Confirmation happens only once: Like a polio vaccination, once a person is confirmed there is no need for it to happen again. The act of confirmation renders the person immune from apostasy. They no longer are required to make another public affirmation of faith. Unlike the physician, the athlete, or the teacher, confirmed adolescents need not "practice" their faith; nor is there a need for refresher courses. Confirmation is sufficient unto itself to ward off any apostasy. Only by invitation does the Church honor requests for renewal of confirmation vows or public affirmations of faith.

Those who fully understand Christian practices know that the faith journey is one of becoming; not one of ever achieving full status as a Christian. The journey is fluid. The seeker is constantly striving for awareness and fulfillment. Perhaps confirmation needs to be a recurring process, an educational venture that happens periodically throughout one's life, regularly from cradle to grave.

Confirmation completes baptism: Despite that many congregations treat confirmation as a sacrament they all know it isn't. It is an affirmation of a sacrament. It has no sacramental validly by its self. What is lost as a sacrament, however, is made up with pomp and circumstance. Congregations like celebrations and they treat confirmation as a fête. It is a "coming of age" celebration and most congregations acknowledge this in grand fashion. There is the worship experience, confirmation dinner, presents, white gowns, flowers, parties. No other occasion of the congregation (except perhaps a wedding) receives such elaborate attention. But the hoopla attached to the occasion only adds to the adolescent's assumption that it is a graduation. For the congregation it legitimizes baptism. For the teen, it is a termination of an educational process. Neither the teen nor the Church members are under the illusion that the confirmand now fully understands the Christian faith.

Pastors will teach the confirmation class: No argument here. Despite how many advanced degrees they have earned or how well versed in biblical narratives they are or how strong and vital their commitment to the principles of the Christian faith, lay persons seem never qualified to teach confirmation. Just because they don't have a "theological" degree, it's assumed they are not competent. This is more a self-assessment by a hesitant congregation than it is a fact of genuine qualifications.

"It's the pastor's responsibility, that's why we hired him." I have known many pastors otherwise very qualified, but who simply do not have the personality or the temperament to teach. Besides, they don't particularly like adolescents. They might be excellent spiritual advisors to adults, but can be greatly annoying to teenagers. Since we place such emphasis upon confirmation as the definitive faith formation tool for adolescents, we should be seeking out the best qualified people, lay or clergy, as instructors. The teacher must like adolescents.

Confirmands will become church members: It is assumed; strongly encouraged, and expected, that confirmands will join the church. Confirmation is the initiation into church membership. Upon completion of the catechism and confirmed by the congregation, students are invited to join the church. Invited is an understatement. The confirmand is reminded that membership is a personal decision but despite allowing for choice, considerable pressure is put of the student by pastors, parents, and sometimes even by peers. Church membership is assumed as the logical outcome of confirmation.

Not all adolescents are mature enough, however, to assume the responsibilities of church membership. As new members and as a gesture of welcoming, congregations often ask new confirmands to become members of one or another of the Church's committees of which they have little knowledge and even less interest. Adolescents don't work well on committees. And then we wonder why they become scarce and stay away from church activities.

Denominational history is required: At some point during the class sessions, and usually for a longer period than necessary, denominational history is studied. Studied is not the optional term; rather the student is exposed whether they are paying attention or not, to the church's denominational founding and history. The denomination's history takes priority because it is the denomination that produced the curriculum. Students show little interest in this history, probably less than the history recited in their school curriculum. History is just not the "thing" that adolescents' find interesting. I suspect that most adolescents have no idea what a denomination is, what its relationship is to the local church, and could care less.

Mission projects are mandatory: Confirmation is not just a head trip, it's also hands-on. More so in the past decade, mission awareness has taken on an element of priority for the confirmation student. We anticipate that if the student is exposed to "mission;" serving others in some fashion or another, the student will better understand the practices of the Christian faith about generosity, empathy, peace and justice. No better way to learn than by direct participation. These mission endeavors need not be elaborate trips to foreign lands. Service can focus on local needs and concerns, toward people in low income neighborhoods, with culturally deprived kids, with local food banks, and as volunteers with already established service organizations such as the Salvation Army.

The intent of service projects is acculturate them to develop a Christian perspective of generosity and service. Unfortunately, I have often heard student remarks, upon returning from a low income inner-city neighborhood, "I'm glad I don't have to live like that." Sympathies are expressed about the plight of the poor, but no commitment to economic justice nor budding relationship with the disadvantaged occur. This is not an indictment of mission with adolescents; rather it is a cautionary disclaimer to be aware that the intended purpose is easily subverted. The leader needs to be astute about how mission trips affect changing attitudes.

Week-end retreats are a necessity: It's inevitable. Nothing builds community better than a week-end retreat; lodged away in some nearby retreat center with bunk beds. a common mess hall, a single bathroom, and plenty of open space beside a woods where the kids can hide. It needs to be some distance from parents. Each year of my ministry I swore that I would spend no more than an hour at a time with a group of raging adolescents and each year I end up leading a week-end retreat with confirmation students. What was I thinking? I convinced myself that retreats build relationships, encourage trustfulness, and focus attention on the Church's mission of community building. All of these are admirable goals for adolescents but not necessarily the same goals the teens have for themselves. Student's goals include such attributes as getting away from parents, meeting friends in the woods, and staying up as late as possible. If such actions heighten relationships and encourage community building, it's by accident not by intention.

Retreats can serve a purpose, but it takes detailed planning to achieve goals and divert disasters. One disgruntled parent commented on the following:

> *"Our parish's confirmation program includes two years of worthless ("exploring your dreams") classes, and then a nonnegotiable mandatory weekend sleep-over retreat. My son went on the retreat and had to deal with a room full of teenage boys at night telling dirty stories and teasing him for not wanting to look at photos of women in a car magazine. Also, the girls in their pajamas (do you know what teenage girls wear for pajamas?!) were mixing with the boys." (Jimmy Akin.com).*

Parents promise to be supportive: Teens do not choose to participate in confirmation with the same enthusiasm they choose to participate in baseball leagues, football practice, school clubs, or even piano lessons. They participate because their parents insist. Parents sign up their kids for confirmation. They promise to have them there for each session, on time, and with homework completed. They also promise to help with program details, provide refreshments as needed, come to parent's orientations, drive kids to retreats and chaperone mission trips. But then the family vacation is scheduled. Soccer games happen on Wednesday evenings, and school work with extra tutoring is necessary. All these activities conflict with confirmation. There seems always to be some legitimate excuse for absences. What should a parent do? Wednesday evening and Sunday mornings are the expected time for confirmation. Conflicts arise and interfere no matter what day or time. Accept this, but don't be afraid to use the congregation's expectations for confirmation as leverage for insisting that those who commit to the program follow through.

Confirmation is always completed: Not ever student will successfully complete the requirements for confirmation, but every student who begins the program will pass, graduate, and be invited to join the church. This being the case, I wonder why confirmation education at all. From comments made by parents and other church members, the "real" purpose of confirmation is to guarantee fresh membership, with or without adequate preparations. No parent wants his/her child to "fail" confirmation.

Shame on us, the congregation, for not providing adequate teaching. It can't be the student's fault, it must be a lack of responsibility on the part of the pastor or whoever did the teaching. The congregation "passes" all who begin the program, despite not completing it, so as not to embarrass the family and to assure a decent flock of new members.

Confirmation serves a useful purpose: Polls indicate the majority of pastors and church members are optimistic about confirmation despite claiming it can often be useless. When acknowledged as useful, however, it is not defined by acknowledging any change in the student's attitude or growth in their faith formation. Rather, it is a manifestation that the student has "struggled" through a year of confirmation. That alone is deserving of acceptance and acknowledgment. Most importantly, they have decided to join the church to the great delight of the congregation. Many pastors shrug at this thought and contend that the challenges of knowing the basic tenets of the faith were ignored or slighted in favor of attempts to convince the kids of the relevance of church membership

Just because we have "always done it that way" need not mean it is the best or the worst. I am sure that some of the activities that are traditionally associated with confirmation are helpful, but just as many are worn out and need to be replaced. The point being is that there are many common denominators that occur among most Protestant congregations.

One final thought. It is interesting, if not revealing, that few if any nondenominational evangelical churches include confirmation as one of their activities for teenagers. A survey of large, mega-churches reveals expansive youth ministry programs involving hundreds of teenagers, but no mention of confirmation. I suspect that since they do not claim to be part of any traditional denomination, they are not pressured and feel no obligation to include confirmation. And yet the appeal of these congregations to teenagers and their families is phenomenal. This suggests that confirmation may continue to be a program of mainline churches because of tradition rather than purpose.

2

MAMA, DON'T LET YOUR BABIES GROW UP TO BE APOSTATES

"Awarness of our beliefs creates
security in our stance"

--Carl Trueman

Sometimes you have to be careful what you wish for. A case in point. A few years ago while I was still teaching a confirmation class, I thought it would be enlightening to include some of the students during morning worship service. My intent was for them to share their wisdom about the Christian faith, their beliefs and practices, that I had worked so hard teaching them over the past nine months. They would do well and make me proud. That was my wish.

Sitting as a group in front of the sanctuary, dressed in their best, they looked prepared. I was to act as monitor during a question and answer segment of the service. The congregation looked expectant. These were their sons and daughters, the future of our church. It started off well.

"Let's begin with each of you sharing a bit of what you believe about your Christian faith," I announced. "Jamie, can you talk about what you believe about God?"

"Well..., um...., I believe God is good, maybe even great," She began. "I think God lives in heaven and if I act good then when I die, I'll get to heaven with God."

There was a pause. I thought she was thinking about adding some more profound thoughts derived from the many class sessions where we discussed the Christian creeds, our beliefs about the mystery and grace of God, and God's acts of redemption. When her pause became too long, I interrupted.

"Anything else you want to add?" I asked her.

"No. That's about it."

One student after another shared thoughts about God. None of them went beyond the insightful and thoughtful words expressed by Jamie. By the conclusion of worship, I was feeling depressed. Had I completely failed these students? What was the congregation thinking?

I stood in the doorway greeting worshippers as they exited. "Enjoyed the service, pastor. Really done a good job with the confirmation kids."

Then another comment. "We have a group of bright kids here. They really know their Christian stuff."

Overwhelmingly the response was positive. They thought the students well informed, committed, and ready to become responsible church members. Well why not. They were clones of their parents.

The book of Proverbs gives advice about child-rearing. *"Train up a child in the way he should go, and when he is old, he will not depart from it"* (Prov. 22:6 RSV). Not all training turns out as expected. Somewhere between birth and adulthood all hell breaks loose. We call the worst of this in-between state adolescence. In some ways, the teenage years provide a spiritual awakening. Physical, emotional and intellectual changes converge as the teen begins the autonomous years; a time for making choices. Unfortunately, searching for spiritual identity is least among these choices. Despite being a part of a Christian community, with some exceptions, teenagers appear uninformed and unacquainted, and even worse, without curiosity about their religious beliefs and faith practices.

She was among the most articulate teenagers I had ever encountered. Though only fourteen, she expressed herself without hesitation and with authority and confidence. She was my "prize" student in confirmation, never missed a class and had an opinion on every subject. Unfortunately she dominated discussions, but was insightful and knowledgeable about the Christian faith and her beliefs in God.

She sat in my office. "I just can't feel any warmth about my faith in God anymore," she told me. "Yeah…I learned a lot about God and I think I know what's in the bible, but I don't love it like I used to."

To become a Christian it takes passion. This teenager, like so very many I have met, has undergone a transformation. Her passion for religion and God dissolved as she passed through adolescence. She intentionally disavowed her faith. No longer was it a priority in her life. At least she knew something about her faith. In this, she was unique. Most teenagers never know enough about their faith to have something to disavow.

> *"Most of us became Christian by looking over someone else's shoulders, emulating some admired older Christian, taking up a way of life that was made real and accessible through the witness of someone else. So, while books, films, and lectures could be used for confirmation class, they should only supplement the main task of putting young Christians in close proximity with older Christian mentors who invite these younger Christians to look over their shoulders as they both attempt to live as Christians."*
>
> (*Christian Century*, March 16, 1988, p.17 used by permission).

> *"No Christian parent wants to hear the words 'apostasy' and 'my child' uttered in the same sentence, or the very thought that our children may be falling away from Christianity is - or should be – terrifying."*
>
> --Ed Vitagliano, "Are Our Churchgoing Youth Falling Away from Faith," Agape Press quoted in Christianity.com

God, religion...whatever.

At least once each decade, researchers, pollsters, sociologists, and other inquisitive folk descend upon the teenage population of America in droves hoping to elicit the latest adolescent attitudes, beliefs, and behaviors. The public harbors a deep fascination and curiosity about the mindset of teenagers and wonders about their impact upon culture. For some inquiring adults it represents a genuine interest in knowing what the future holds. For others, I suspect, it is an exercise in nostalgia.

I am not sure why adolescents are fair game for spying and analysis, but I suspect that they are an enigma to most adults. Perhaps it is the fear of the unknown. They worry that the teens are hiding something from them and they want to know what that is. This apprehension causes adults anxiety and distress about teenagers.

Those who study teenagers are prolific and unrestrictive in their focus. Every aspect of teenage culture is open for scrutiny – relationships, sex, music, parents, peers, and ethical attitudes both positive and negative. Not to be ignored as peripheral is the arena of religion. Considerable research during the past decade has centered on teenage perceptions of religious conviction.

During the years between 2003 – 2005 under the auspices of the National Study of Youth and Religion (NSYR), literally dozens of trained researchers, mostly associated with sociological studies, were unleashed to query thousands of American teenagers (ages 13-17) of all faiths and persuasions; Catholics, liberal and conservative Protestants, Jewish, Islam, LDS, and others. Their intention was to uncover what teenagers really thought about religious beliefs and practices. Their findings were presented in the book, *Soul Searching, the Religious and Spiritual Lives of American Teenagers* by Christian Smith and Melinda Denton (Oxford University Press, 2005), by Christian Smith and Melinda Lundquist Denton. Contributing to the dialogue concerning the findings was Kenda Creasy in her book *Almost Christian:*

What the Faith of Our Teenagers is Telling the American Church (Oxford University Press, 2010)

It's not a pretty picture. The read can be most disturbing. Nearly every aspect imaginable concerning teenage religious beliefs and practices is examined and analyzed along with potential implications for the faith formation of adolescents.

"We talked with teens," Smith states in the book, "about what they get enthusiastic about, what pressing issues concern them at this time in their lives." According to Smith and Denton, most mentioned friends and peer relationships, drug use and abuse, sex, music, family relationships, and other similar subjects of interest to teens. Rarely arising in these conversations were teenage religious queries. They had no religious identities other than to be able to name the church to which their family belonged. Religion did not appear to hold much importance or have any significant bearing toward what matters to them at the present time.

The dumbing down of faith.

Teenage perceptions of God give rise to a simplistic and self-centered characterization of God. As suggested by Smith and Denton and summarized by Kenda Dean, the mantra of teenage beliefs consists of the following characteristics

- God does exist. God created the world but that's about it.
- God does not involve himself in daily activities, unless asked.
- God wants people to be nice, responsible moral beings.
- God wants people to feel good about themselves.
- God invites the good people to live in heaven after death.

These responses to the nature of God remind me of the Boy Scout motto. If God requires anything at all from people, it's that they become good boy scouts – "A scout is trustworthy, loyal, helpful, friendly, courteous, kind, obedient, cheerful, thrifty, brave, clean and reverent."

> *"...the vast majority of them (teenagers) to be incredibly inarticulate about their faith, their religious beliefs and practices, and its meaning or place in their lives."*
>
> (*Soul Searching*, Smith and Denton, quoted by Ed Vitagliano, Agape Press, reproduced in the AFA Journal, Jan., 2006)

This "articulation problem" is not an indication that teens have no faith nor does it imply that they get tongue-tied about all matters of their lives. The NSYR study reports that a majority of teens claim a faith in the Christian tradition, but the tenets of that faith are not consistent with or remotely akin to traditional Christian theology. Instead their faith beliefs and practices tend to mirror their parent's faith, which proved to be overly simplistic.

> *"Talking explicitly about sex is easy for MTV-watching teens. Using a word like sin is much harder."*
>
> (*Jesus Isn't Cool* by Channon Ross, Christian Century, Sept. 6, 2005, p.23 used by permission.)

Talk with teens about school, peers, friends, sex, or family and they will open up and express attitudes with great insight. Their reluctance appears to pertain to religious matters exclusively. This unusual problem suggests a number of possibilities. (1) Teens either don't know how or don't want to talk about their religious faith and practices because they have never been encouraged to do so. Research shows neither parents nor local congregations spend any significant time in dialogue with teens about matters of faith. (2) Teens have accepted a set of religious beliefs that are so dissimilar from traditional tenets of Christian faith as to be unrecognizable They may mumble on about their faith, but adults haven't a clue as to what they actually believe. Kenda Dean, an astute examiner of American teen faith practices, notes that the faith proclaimed by today's teens is *"...a religious outlook that is quite distinct from Christianity, Judaism, Islam, or any of the world's major religions (that) helps people be nice, feel good, and leaves God in the background."* (*Almost Christian*, p.21 by permission of Oxford University Press). (3) There is a third explanation that can't be totally dismissed and might have some merit. Can it be that teens may just find great delight in bucking the beliefs and religious practices of the adult generation? It can be frustrating to watch teens fracture relationships and traditions in pursuit of independence. This would not be the first time.

According to the NSYR report, many teens do maintain a wholesome relationship with the church. They acknowledge appreciation for their congregations, find them to be welcoming and nurturing places, and establish meaningful relationships with both adults and peers in these communities. But beyond these friendly associations, teens have little or no interest toward exploring their faith. The members of the congregations reciprocate with activities, support for youth ministry, funds for mission travel, and facilities for sports and games, but ask them to teach the basic tenets of the Christian faith and they dissolve into the corners. They may be as much in the dark about these tenets as the very teens they need to teach.

Most commentators reacting to the work presented in *Soul Searching* (Smith and Denton) sum up the findings of teenaged religious beliefs with the following set of characteristics. Teens tend to have the following perceptions and religion exists to:

Allow the person to feel good.

Encourage people to be nice.

Support the idea of doing good things.

Self-improvement.

Become successful.

According to the researchers, all of the above are primary features of the content of religious beliefs and practices of American teenagers. To say they are simplistic is an understatement.

George Barna summed up the different faith of teenagers with the single word, "*whatever*, which is nothing more than a shrug of the shoulders at the thought of absolute truth."

What appears to be the dominant religion among teenagers has it's foundations in popular attitudes; feeling good, happy, and secure. It's about attaining subjective peace, being able to solve problems, particularly through prayer, and getting along with others.

Contrary to popular assumptions, the religion of American teens, according to the prevailing research, is particularly conventional. These adolescents are not "seekers"; they do not strive for insight and understanding of their faith or other faiths but are content with the faith inherited from their parents. "This is how my family does it," one teen responded when asked why she was a Christian and what did it mean to her. "I am happy and it's good enough for me."

Religion is not a big deal for teenagers. They are quite willing to imitate the religious beliefs and practices of their parents. This attitude contrasts sharply from that of just a few decades ago. While I was growing up, my parent's greatest fear was that I would become a hippie, move to Southern California, smoke pot, and become a Buddhist; a rejection of everything they stood for. I was part of the beat generation, encouraged by the likes of Timothy Leary to "turn on and drop out." Our generation rebelled against everything the establishment proclaimed and religion was no exception.

Imagine my surprise when learning that "what goes around comes around." My own children became very accepting of the "establishment" and even participated in Sunday school willingly. Their "curiosity" about religious matters was less than overwhelming despite their father being an ordained pastor.

What the research did not discover among the teenaged population interviewed was any sense that religion summons people to embrace obedience to truth regardless of personal consequences or reward. Teens adhere to a laissez-faire, let live attitude. Truth for me and truth for you, each is valid. There is no universal truth. Each person decides for himself; if it works for you, fine.

Most teens are liberal and accepting of religious pluralism in America. This does not mean that they are aware of the tenets and practices of other faiths and, upon examination, found them to be acceptable. Rather, they appear as ignorant of other faiths to the same degree they are ignorant of their own. *"Don't make me talk about my faith and I won't make you tell me about yours."* For the teen, because religion matters little, therefore it matters little what faith another person has.

Adolescents approach issues of religion and faith practices from a subjective perspective. Faith is a means for helping people get through life as happy as possible. In this sense, teens count on faith much like a client counts on the therapist. Largely, the greatest disappointment found among the beliefs and practices of American teens is their unwillingness or inability to express attitudes about faith practices openly. Because they are so inarticulate, it is difficult to know what they believe. To conclude that they have inadequate beliefs about their Christian faith may be a bit presumptuous. The research found that most teens acknowledge that nobody, not their parents, their peers, or their congregation ever asks them to talk about their faith. If we don't listen to them speak of faith issues, we are hard pressed to fully comprehend what's happening inside their heads.

When prompted, the largest proportion of teens indicate that their faith and practices are basically the same or similar to their parents. Parents have the greatest influence on teens, if not in all social matters, at least in faith formation. As one commentator suggests, *"youth today have more in common with grownups than not. They have embraced mainstream values. Their main concern is to succeed in the society that has been given to them."* Like father, like son.

Educational contributions of the congregation.

Despite its ability to attract adolescents and its elaborate educational programs, the church contributes little toward creating an authentic faith. It is more concerned with the numbers of teens it attracts through games, retreats, and mission projects than with the depth and quality of the faith it helps form. Numbers make a difference.

The teaching curriculums have fuzzy goals and are often without clear purposes. Instead they are meanderings of bible stories suitable for telling children combined with a host of simplistic activities designed to keep students busy. Even the best of the best curriculums do little more than to dumb down the biblical teachings to make them age appropriate. As Kenda Dean suggests, *"What if the blasé religiosity of most American teenagers is not the result of poor communications, but the result of excellent communication of a watered-down gospel so devoid of God's giving love in Jesus Christ ...that it might not be Christianity at all?"(Almost Christian,* p.12 by permission of Oxford University Press)

Who is to blame? It would be easy to blame the church or synagogue. Their teaching methods must be lax. They don't know how to communicate with teenagers. That may be too simple. Some pundits reply just the opposite. They contend that catechism may lax but churches employ an excellent strategy of asserting that "faith matters little." that Christianity is not a big deal. Just get the kids into membership and all will work itself out.

Despite its inadequacies, there continues to exist a universal program of Confirmation education. Hardly a congregation subsists, with the exception of evangelical, conservative churches, which do not involve their adolescents in a program of some sort leading to confirmation. At its core, confirmation education intends to enhance faith formation; to create an augmented understanding of the Christian faith and its practices for adolescents. Indeed, most of the kids have progressed through church school and are familiar with many of the traditional bible stories and can recite them from memory. But confirmation is more than recitation of bible stories. It proposes to be that period in adolescent faith formation that introduces kids to the basic tenets of their faith and challenges them to consider the meaning and significance. From what we know and observe, however, confirmation in most of our Protestant congregations falls far short of this ideal. As a consequence, the teens of this generation grow up without a consequential faith.

For the serious confirmation educator, these attitudes signify that the atmosphere for teenage faith formation is not entirely absent or closed. It does not mean the obstacles that can't be overcome. It presents a challenge, difficult at the very least, but still a viable option. Instead we can conclude that teenagers might possibly be open to faith nurturing, despite not having any knowledge of their own, if we can determine appropriate and skillful teaching methods. Remember, teens have already told us that the reason they don't inquire about religious matters is that nobody asks them; no one wants to engage them in this type of dialogue. Confirmation is the proper place for this conversation to happen. So start talking.

3

INCLUDED OR NOT

Baptism, Confirmation and the Quest for Age Relevance

"In my opinion, it has always been a spiritual and moral imperative that all of God's children, any person, men and women alike, feel I have access, I am included in the ideals and tradition of our faith, whatever that faith may be. Humanity is created in the likeness of God without exception. All humanity has the right embraced fully."

---Rabbi Howard Morrison,
quoted by Marie Lewis at *Marielewis.com*

A small girl sits beside her mother during worship. The ushers are about to pass the Eucharistic plate with consecrated bread down the aisle where the girl and her mother are sitting. As it approaches, the girl reaches out to take a piece of bread. Suddenly an elderly man sitting directly behind the girl leans forward, grabs her hand, and in a whispered voice remarks, "You have to wait till you are older, honey, after you are confirmed." The mother looks puzzled, but says nothing. Feeling intimidated, the girl withdraws her hand. The plate passes on to the next person.

This congregation baptized the little girl as an infant. She attends Sunday school regularly. She goes with her mother to the worship service following Sunday school. Mom is confused. She has been to other churches of the same denomination and watched kids her daughter's age receive the communion elements. She decides to query the pastor after the service.

"Why can't Marie take communion here?" she asks the pastor.

"Well actually she is allowed," he responds. "It's just that many of the older members still hang onto the notion that communion be offered only to kids who have completed confirmation and joined the church."

"Is that attitude going to change?"

"Probably not soon," the pastor responds looking a bit forlorn. He remembers that he is the pastor who baptized Marie a few years back. He then adds, "But I agree with you. Why give birth if you intend to starve the child?"

Confusion and disagreement.

Although not a raging debate, many congregations still suffer confusion and disparity over the administration of the sacrament of communion. Two distinct perspectives appear. On the one hand are those who claim baptism is, in fact, the sacrament of inclusion into the body of Christ. It makes no difference that it occurs in infancy; the child is still fully included in the faith and as such, should be invited to the table.

On the other hand are the more traditionalists who maintain that baptism as an infant only qualifies as "preparatory." Until confirmation is bestowed, a public affirmation is delivered, and the confirmand joins the church, the baptism is not fully completed. The invitation to the table should be withheld until *"after"* that moment.

There is a strong theological belief among most American Protestant congregations that confirmation is an affirmation of one's own baptism. Confirmation has no "standing;" its mere existence is dependent upon baptism. The Presbyterians, who like to use their own language, proclaim that *"confirmation...is deciding for one's self to publically affirm the vows taken on their behalf in baptism as infants".*

The emphasis here is on decision. The reasoning is that infant baptism was done *"to"* the person, while confirmation is done *"by"* the person. Confirmation legitimizes the baptism because it allows adolescents to sanction their baptism. Confirmation is not understood to be a sacrament. Even Catholics and Orthodox Christian's are moving confirmation theologically toward the concept of re-affirmation of baptism. There is growing pressure upon Catholics to view confirmation as "renewable;" something pursued continually throughout one's life time. The problem causing the greatest heart burn for most congregations, Christian or Jewish, is the attitude of graduation; that confirmation causes the teen's promotion out of the church.

Confirmation is not an ending. It is a beginning. It's intention is to be an initiation into the church community. Far too many adolescents, however, complete the course of study, become confirmed by the church, and simply disappear. The debate that swirls around confirmation, communion, and membership in the church, however, is not of great concern to most church-going teenagers. Their intent is to complete the program and get on with their lives.

Confirmation: at what age?

If American teens lack the will and/or curiosity to learn about the basic tenets of the Christian faith, does it really matter what age confirmation happens, or for that matter, whether it happens at all? It would be far easier if the teens simple acquiesced to the religion of their parents and automatically matriculated into the life of the congregation. I am sure this would make teens happier and more content not to mention the aggravation confirmation causes their parents.

To give proper consideration to this question, we first need clarification of the title *"youth"*. The very concept of "youth" needs some re-examination. For the practice of confirmation, the church views youth as the ages of 13-17, primarily the high school years. Once beyond high school, when the person pursues higher education, goes into the military, or locates a job, the church considers the person to be an adult. They are no longer "youth," but rather mature adults. Consequently, the congregation dismisses them and they become "invisible, which for the most part, they are."

But youth is an ambiguous term, not clearly defined or exactly described in American culture. It has only been a hundred years or so that we have had "adolescences." Adolescence is an invented period of life when teenagers serve an ambiguous role. Between the ages of 13 -17 or thereabouts they have no other status then to be students, or minimal wage earners at part time jobs. They can't vote so they have no power to determine their future. They are neither children nor adults; they exist in limbo. So what are they?

They are distinguishable people, whether we like it or not. In ways unbeknownst to adults, they actively participate in determining their present and future. They decide who they are and do so in a number of ways. First of all they choose an identity, rather than have an identity provided for them, which is a cause of grief for their parents. This begins the period adolescent rejection of parental values. Further they define themselves collectively in the phenomenon of youth culture. This culture takes on particular music styles, fashions, and a "youth" language. Adolescents are in constant flux and instability. When the next generation comes along, they re-define these roles all over again but in new terms.

We are never quite sure, however, when childhood ends and adulthood begins. Some sociologists want to expand "youth" by virtue of behavior and attitudes rather than age limits. They indicate the presence of youthfulness that lasts longer then the four years of high school. Many students presently in college and even into their early twenties exhibit the same tendencies attributed to youth – seeking a personal aim in life, searching for self-identity, easily influenced by competing ideas and advertising. Many people in their mid-twenties continue to function as youth. They participate in groups similar to those of much younger people. They live at home with their parents. They rely upon other adults to meet their basic needs just as they did when teenagers.

Sociologists expand the formative years of youthfulness into the early twenties while the church hangs on to the specific parameters of high school.

Meanwhile the church continues to consider youth at the traditional ages of 13-17. They contend those are spiritually formative years, which they are, but not exclusively for all young people. Part of the problem of teenage apostasy is the insistence of the church upon focusing primary attention on this age, with no follow up in the latter stages of "youthfulness." If confirmation education expands beyond adolescences it would capture the curiosity of mature students rather than depending upon an immature younger age.

The crux of the discussion focuses on the concept of "formative "years. At what age is the person most likely to comprehend and seek out spiritual growth? If the formative years extend upward, it makes sense to include faith formation learning as part of those expanded years; the time after high school. At present, most churches cease learning opportunities for people above the high school age, partly because of their nonattendance at church. This absence of faith related activities for older youth only encourages the concept that confirmation was a graduation; no more religious instruction or practice needed. If confirmation continues as a "graduation", there is little incentive for further learning. People in their early twenties are just as susceptible as teenagers about being "inarticulate" toward their religious beliefs and faith practices.

Martin Copenhaver, in an article entitled *What's Confirmation For?* (Christian Century, June 2, 2009) advocates that teenagers probably have no conception of *"eternal matters"*, much less the capacity to make sense of the Christian theology. He maintains that it might be a waste of time and resources to think about faith formation with adolescents. Following his article, the next issue of the Century provided feedback from many who disagreed with Copenhaver. *"Maybe we need to be more interested in the confirmation essays (of teenagers) and not less so,"* writes Carl F Schultz. *"Not all reflections upon the Christian life need be exercises in narcissism. If they were, there would be no place for using the ancient creedal formulas ...to witness to the faith and its impact upon our personal lives"* (Christian Century, June 9, 2009 used by permission).

There is ample evidence, however, that the more mature the person the greater the interest and ability to comprehend religious faith. The Church of the Latter Day Saints (Mormons) is cited as an example. Dr. Kenda Creasy Dean has acknowledged some significant differences between young adults from the LDS church and those teenagers from mainline churches. In addition to the age difference being slightly older, these differences are due to "*...core theological convictions that add up to a consequential faith" for LDS young people. LDS youth are taught or inspired by:*

> *1.Their traditions have a creed or God-story.*
> *2.(They) belong to a community that enacts the God-story.*
> *3.They feel called by this story to contribute to a larger purpose*
> *4.They have hope for the future promised by this story.*
>
> *In addition these youth...have families and churches that model-convincingly-that these tools matter."*
>
> (*Almost Christian*, p. 49 by permission of Oxford University Press)

Dr. Dean does not proposes that LDS students are more religious or moral than others, only that they have incorporated the above characteristics as part of the religious nurture. The incorporation of these principles occurs at a more mature age than traditional confirmation She also posits that Mormons capitalize on these characteristics to encourage enthusiasm among youth toward their belief systems.

We might balk when the Mormon youth come knocking on our doors right at dinner time, but we can't argue with their "spiritually significant" attitudes. These missionaries are working on a program that connects them to their faith commitment for a life time. Most of these students are over the high school age which lends credence to the proposition that confirmation as a faith formation process might fare better if introduced at a later age.

The process of becoming Christian.

In another part of this book, we will talk about Christian construction; that becoming a Christian is a process full of enquiry, investigation, and analyses. As such, it certainly can't be restricted to one age bracket to the exclusion of all other ages and stages of life. Like a Rolls Royce automobile that constantly needs fine tuning and a healthy diet of refined fuel to run at its best, so also can a case be made that each Christian needs to have periodic checkups, adjustments, and fine tuning of their vows of baptism. Faith formation needs continual refueling. The age of the person has little bearing on faith formation. It is far better to make a judgment on the person's maturity level. Faith formation is a developmental experience. By necessity, the student must be "emotionally and mentally" ready

Understanding the developmental stages of the adolescent is imperative. It is probably a waste of time and energy to expect a 13 year old adolescent to express interest in "matters of religion" much less comprehend them beyond being able to recite biblical stories recalled from Church school. Because we continue to infuse adolescents with religious beliefs and practices which are beyond their comprehension and way over their heads, we contribute to, not decrease, the confirmation graduation rate.

There appears to be merit in "staged" confirmation programs. Following the developmental paradigm, confirmation can begin at one age and completed at another. Faith formation happens in stages, not all at once. First started in 7th grade or thereabout, repeated two years later, and completed in 12th grade or beyond Teenagers go through different stages of faith formation just as they go through different stages of personal development. The virtue lies in repetition; the principals of Christian formation are presented to students in stages as they grow in maturity. Each age and stage of maturity brings the ability to more fully understand the meaning and significance of baptism, as well as the tenets of the faith.

Confirmation in phases.

One author (*Confirmation: Presbyterian Practices in Ecumenical Perspective* by Richard R. Osmer, pp.200-201) suggests a two phase process for confirmation independent of age. To be confirmed is not a matter of a once in a life time individual decision. Rather it is the role of the congregation to fully accept that confirmation is a re-affirmation of baptism and to encourage this action along every step of the person's faith journey.

Faith journeys need mentors of differing kinds. The first mentor can be the pastor. Once the decision is made by all involved (student and congregation) that confirmation is an ongoing, repeatable process whether for the first or fifth time, the pastor meets with the candidate. This is not a judgment call but rather a time to encourage questioning about the implications of faith for the candidate. Dialogue revolves around the following:

- Why are you seeking confirmation now?
- Do you feel well grounded in your basic beliefs and are you still open to growth in faith?
- Are there aspects of your faith you especially want to pursue?
- Do you understand the meaning of confirmation?

These questions are adjusted depending upon the age, but they are all open ended and meant to inspire some "articulation" on the part of the confirmand despite the age or stage in life.

The second phase involves the choice of a spiritual mentor; an experienced guide or trusted counselor. It is important this NOT be the pastor. The mentor need not be a theologian. The mentor's role is to be in dialogue with the conformant, encourage exploration of faith matters, and serve as sponsor as appropriate. Spiritual mentors advocate in the same way as addiction mentors – support. Both experiences can be long and arduous journeys filled with misgivings, uncertainties, and hesitations but well worth the effort.

Mentors walk a fine line between dispensing concrete guidance in faith practices and encouraging experimentation in finding patterns that work for the conformant. Mentors need to be present to the conformant, able to counter doubts and uncertainties, and be accepting of the struggles accompanying faith formation.

Mentors are active in the congregation. They attend worship. They pray regularly. They participate in mission and service. They are models for the confirmand. I am reminded of William Willimons image of what he wished for the confirmation class he taught; "*that each confirmand turn out to be like Mr. Black,*" an admired Christian who fulfilled all the responsibilities of being a person of faith. Mentors help eliminate drop outs, particularly among high school teenagers.

No conclusions appear forthcoming concerning the appropriate age to either begin or end the confirmation quandary. Despite the evidence that supports newer models, the majority of congregations still choose middle adolescence, identifying that age as being able to "*Imagine the possibilities. Middle adolescents are in the concrete thinking stage, but (still) able to deal with abstract ideas and hypothetical situations, which makes theologizing possible.*" (*Confirmation and Baptismal Affirmation,* Robert Brown and Roy Freed, 1994).

Trends in confirmation education.

Pastors, in particular, are proposing that confirmation be led away from simple knowledge of the fundamentals of the Christian faith in a non-subjective manner– doctrinal positions around sin, salvation, Christ, inerrancy of the bible, the church, the Holy Spirit, human nature and destiny – and toward dealing with the subject matter (doctrine) more subjectively and personally in such a way as to enable students to access the truth of doctrine in terms of their own frame of references.

Mark Hinds explains this well. (*Teaching for Responsibility; Confirmation and the Book of Proverbs,* Religious Education, Spring 1998). Hinds suggest that religious teaching, particularly as it relates to what is happening in confirmation of adolescents, follows one of two paths. (1) as approved storytelling of the community's lore or (2) as a sympathetic manager/therapist that attends to the becoming Christian of young people. This may best be illustrated in the debate between Richard Osmer and the authors of the confirmation series *Journey's in Faith* (Journeys in faith, 20 S. Main Street, Janesville, WI).

Osmer contends that confirmation education would better serve adolescents by "harking back to traditional forms of catechetical instruction." Osmer emphasizes content and authoritative teaching. Knowing the basic doctrines of the Christian faith is of primary concern. Osmer does not address the problem of inexperience and disinterest of teenagers toward beliefs and practices

By contrast, the authors of *Journey's In Faith* promote confirmation education that is most appropriately concerned with teenage self-discovery as persons of faith. *Journey's In Faith* primarily stress therapeutic discourse focusing on the concerns for the teenager. Doctrine is not without purpose but only as it informs the way the person makes life decisions in accord with Christian faith.

Neither method is without controversy. Osmer is accused of excessive moralizing. The traditionalists tread a thin line between imparting information and imposing moral judgments. The traditionalist calls into question the ability of the teenager to make sense of religion under circumstances where the learner has no knowledge of basic beliefs.

On the other hand, *Journey's In Faith* is accused of turning learning into a bull session of the uninformed. *Journey's In Faith,* by contrast, maintains that testable knowledge of religious beliefs is not as important as asking the question of what difference it makes in one's life. The emphasis is upon understanding beliefs only well enough to relate them to the wider response of faith relevant to making healthy decisions about daily experience. Christian beliefs become ethical imperatives; a set of values used to measure good and bad behavior, right decisions, and purposeful judgments.

With the manager/therapist model for confirmation, the educator seeks to create "Christian community" rather than legalistic programs (Browning and Reed, p.140). What is intended for the teenager is the development of relationships, imaginative forms of caring, and discovery of the power of the Christian style of life (Browning and Reed, p.140). The student expects to identify with a life centered in Christ (discipleship) within the community (the church) which is seeking to be the body of Christ working in the world. The manager/therapist model; does not mean that beliefs are taboo for discussion. It does imply, however, that Christian beliefs are open to scrutiny. The student is encouraged to question what difference they make in adjusting to life and faith.

The arguments continue. Neither approach addresses the central problem of religious beliefs nor faith practices of teenagers. The Christian faith upon which the curriculum depends is not a faith that teenagers either know or care about. Any approach to confirmation must include some pragmatic experiences that help the adolescent connect with the tenets of the Christian faith. Without awareness and some comprehension of traditional Christian theology, both teaching methods are fruitless endeavors.

All adolescents, with or without confirmation, have basic developmental needs which must be satisfied no matter what model of teaching is employed. Teenagers have the need to belong (acceptance), the need for forgiveness, the need for independence, and the need for generosity. These needs complement the acceptance of religious beliefs. If we are to focus on the faith formation of teenagers we need to recognize that a head full of doctrine is without value if it excludes these basic needs. But we also need to recognize that without some basic understanding of beliefs and doctrine, we will continue to graduate inarticulate teenagers who perpetuate the situation described by Smith and Denton in *Soul Searching*. For the uninformed, it becomes a dilemma; one where you can't win for losing.

Regardless of the methods utilized, there is an ongoing necessity for faith conversations to happen. Dialogue, once again proves to be an excellent teaching tool despite the age or stage of the learner.

4

CREEDAL THINKING

"Awareness of our beliefs creates security in our stance."

-Carl Trueman

In her book, *(Almost Christian),* Kenda Creasy Dean proposes that a *consequential faith* begins with a *conversational faith.* If persons can't talk about what they believe, then the strength of their beliefs are open to question. From the NSYR study, we learn that *"things can only be so real if we can't articulate them."* Here is the essence of the problem. Articulating faith concerns appears to lay beyond the reach of teens. They must learn how to talk about faith if it is to develop into something meaningful.in their lives.

In a piece written for the *Confirmation Project, "Why I am Part of the Confirmation Project" (July 20, 2014)* Dr. Kenda Dean, a United Methodist teacher and professor at Princeton Theological School, comments on her impression while in confirmation class. She writes:(used with author's permission.)

"If you had been a fly on the wall of Rev. Bergstresser's office back in 1972, you would have been pretty sure that I was one of those confirmands who just wasn't going to make it. My memories of those six mind-numbing Wednesday nights in the pastor's office, sitting in a semi-circle with four other seventh graders around Rev. B's ginormous desk, are mainly of watching the clock for d-e-c-a-d-e-s until Confirmation Class mercifully came to an end."

So how do we remedy this situation? Teens need to talk. Creeds might just provide an answer, or at the very least, be of significant help. If you are a non-Christian, or from certain Christian traditions, including Baptist or Pentecostal, you might be asking, "what exactly is a creed?" Perhaps you know what a creed is, but you find the idea of a creed too formal, too limiting, and stifling. Yet, a creed is not something peculiar or unfamiliar. It is simply a statement of belief, derived from the Latin word *credo*, to believe.

Before you come down too hard on creeds, understand that everyone uses creeds, as does every church/assembly. Even if a group of persons says, "we don't believe in creeds," it obviously does have a creed...its creed is "we don't believe in creeds." Thus, if one has the capacity to believe in something, anything, (even a belief that we do not believe in creeds) one has a creed, even when unspoken. Creeds accurately explain the beliefs of individuals and groups of people often better than the person can explain them. That's why people are drawn to creeds. To avoid conflict, some churches substitute "statements of belief" that are longer and more complicated than the basic Christian creeds, when they want to circumvent the word "creed."

It is a common practice among Protestant congregations that, at some time during the confirmation class preparations, the students write about their faith journey. In those statements, kids make known their beliefs about God, about Jesus, about the Holy Spirit, and about the role of the church in their lives. In too many cases, these statements reveal how little students know or understand about Christian faith. They divulges their inability for articulating their faith.

Thinking that my confirmation methods for teenagers were superior, I engaged the teens in one of my classes to "talk" about their faith. I expected the depth of theology to be shallow, but was completely surprised by the widespread lack of response. It was as if they never were present in class, never heard a word about our common faith and religious practices, never thought what becoming a church member meant. Their responses closely aligned to findings from the NRYS study. The degree of their disinterest was overwhelming.

As noted earlier in an article in the Christian Century, (June 2, 2009 used by permission), the Reverend Martin Copenhaver, who elected to have his confirmation students write statements of faith, remarks that *"typically some statements ...were stumbling attempts to capture these enduring mysteries, while others could only be called statements of doubt. The congregation received each with the lavish appreciation and praise of a parent who was just presented with a child's first drawing"*. Reverend Copenhaver goes on to state he is just not interested in any 15 year olds reflection on eternal matters.

Faith without words.

One conclusion drawn from the National Study on Youth and Religion (*Soul Searching* by Christian Smith and Melina Lundquist Denton, 2009, p. 131) is that the vast majority of teenagers are incredibly inarticulate about their faith, their religious beliefs and practices and its meaning or place in their lives. Knowing this, I was not surprised by the inability or unwillingness of my students to talk about or "articulate" the tenets of their faith. The NSYR study implies that the greater majority of teens will claim the Christian tradition, but the beliefs they hold about that faith have little resemblance to traditional Christian tenets. Instead they attempt to reflect their parent's religious practices, but because even these are foreign to them, even these are rather simplistic.

As indicated earlier talk with teens about school, peers, friends, sex, or family and they will willingly open up and express attitudes with great insight and enthusiasm. Their reluctance appears to pertain to religion exclusively. Their awareness seems to suggest two possibilities. First, as advocated by Kenda Dean in her book *Almost Christian* (1) Teens don't want or don't know how to talk about religious faith and practices because they have never been encouraged to do so. Neither parents nor congregations spend any significant time in dialogue with teens about matters of faith. The researcher George Barna suggest that *teenagers don't think about moral truths often or deeply because they are neither challenged to do so nor is such behavior modeled for them* ("Real Teens" Ch.4, p 92, Regal Books, 2001). Secondly teens have accepted a set of religious beliefs that are so dissimilar from traditional tenets of Christian faith as to be unrecognizable. Ms. Dean concludes that the faith proclaimed by today's teens is "*...a tacit religious outlook that is quite distinct from Christianity, Judaism, Islam, or any of the world's religions (that) helps people be nice, feel good and leaves God in the background*"(Almost Christian,p.21 by permission of Oxford University Press).

According to Dean' interpretation of the NSYR study, religion is not a source of conflict in the lives of teens. They do maintain an appreciation for their local congregation and find church members to be welcoming and nurturing, but as a source of identity, the Christian faith has little influence. This "dumbing down" and "benign whatever-ism" of adolescent religion that Dean and others observe may not be intentional for teens. Rather it's a matter of inheritance. Although teens embrace the religion of their parents without controversy, it is not necessarily because they buy into it, but because they don't consider religion worth arguing about (*Almost Christian,* Appendix B, p. 201).

Enter – The art of creedal thinking.

> *The best way to get most youth involved in and serious about their faith communities is to get their parents more involved in and serious about their faith communities*
>
> (Christian Smith with Melinda Denton, quoted by Kenda Dean in *Almost Christian,* p. 109 by permission of Oxford University Press.)

The above may sound contradictory. On the one hand research indicates that teens generally follow the religious traditions of their parents, but these parents don't have much of a religious tradition to fellow. On the other hand, this same research concludes that teens who embrace a set of religious practices are the very teens whose parents encourage their spiritual involvement is surely referring to parents who have a depth of understanding regarding faith issues.

On any given Sunday morning, millions of Christians recite the words of one creed or statement of faith as part of the worship experience – the Nicene Creed, the Apostles Creed, a denominational statement of faith. Sitting next to these adults are their children with blank stares on their faces. The words they hear sound like a foreign language. I often wonder what goes through the mind of a young person when hearing, "judging the quick and the dead" (Apostles Creed), or the tongue twister, "one holy Catholic and apostolic church" (Nicene Creed). Even the adults admit to a lack of understanding, but take no offense. *"It's always been a part of our worship. I miss it when it is not included."*

Creeds have been around for centuries. Creeds were instituted as a means for aiding us to define and examine what we believe. For religion, they also serve as word symbols of our faith practices. For instance the statement of faith of the United Church of Christ of which I am most familiar uses the following statement as part of its declaration of beliefs. (Used with permission)

> *"You call us into his church to accept the cost and joy of discipleship, to be his servants in the service of men, to proclaim the gospel to all the world and resist the powers of evil, to share in Christ's baptismand eat at his table, to join him in his passion and victory."*

This phrase highlights the action intended by the statement. It symbolizes that being Christian is never easy, that it requires one become a servant, and to participate intentionally in the sacraments.

The word creed comes from the Latin word, "I believe." They reflect many areas for which we attempt to define our beliefs. The framers of the Declaration of Independence created a creed when they chose the words, *"We hold these truths to be self-evident...."* That's what they believed and they so stated. Creeds are particularly appropriate for spiritual expression.

Creeds are testimonies, not tests. They are not examinations for which one has to pass in order to authentic their faith. Creeds don't create beliefs, they reflect them. Creeds don't construct faith, they support it. They don't exhaust the meaning of faith, they enhance it. Creeds are not infallible, they are flexible. Creeds witness to the truth as perceived at that time and in that place.

Because creeds enhance conversational faith; that is to say they are spoken words, they are an excellent tool for use with teenagers. Creeds are spoken. They articulate one's beliefs. What I am proposing is that we focus our teaching and learning in confirmation education on creedal thinking.

Creedal thinking is more than a response in words to beliefs; it is a method of thinking and communicating perceptions of reality. In one sense it is intuitive to the human spirit, i.e. kids articulate beliefs almost from inception. At any age of development creedal thinking can be intentionally taught.

Children form beliefs at very young ages. Whether stated or not, these beliefs reflect their reality of their world. Since they are, and will continue to be, influenced by what they believe, then it makes good educational sense to utilize this format as a means for introducing the tenets of Christian beliefs and practices. First we must demythologize creeds and allow their creation to become as normal as speaking for teenagers.

Crocodiles and creeds.

My daughter once believed that crocodiles lived under her bed. She refused to sleep there until I found a way to remove them. I became exasperated and frustrated over her refusal to believe they existed only in her imagination. This went on for many nights. My wife and I lost sleep because she kept coming into our room in the middle of the night insisting "there are crocodiles under my bed." Finally, after depleting all other options, I took a shoe from the closet, went to her room, and banged it repeatedly on the floor under her bed.

"There, "I told her, "I killed them all."

Once she believed they were all dead and gone, she had no more trouble staying asleep in her own bed.

Crocodiles living under the bed may not qualify as a creed, but her strongly held belief greatly affected her perspective on reality. She was convinced of their existence and stated as much with enthusiasm and conviction. Her "creed" or belief was very powerful and dominated her behavior.

Consider the many beliefs we held as children, perhaps not creeds, but closely resembling them. We were convinced at one time or another of the truth of the following:

- Chocolate milk comes from brown cows.
- Pee turns a different color in swimming pools.
- Thunder is the sound of God bowling.
- Eating bread crust makes your hair curly.
- You must hold your breath passing a cemetery or you'll die.

Teens outgrow childish thinking, but they soon latch on to new beliefs affecting their thinking and behavior forcefully. In such matters as peer relationships, use and abuse of substances, making and maintaining friends, and family conflicts, teenagers have little difficulty stating what they believe; and sharing what's important to them. Ask them to pontificate about these subjects and they will not hesitate to state strongly held beliefs and defend them. They use these "creeds" with knowing.

Their consequent behavior bears this out. The beliefs they hold about these subjects are extremely important but are constantly changing as does their behavior based upon these changed beliefs. At any one time, these beliefs feel like universal truths to the teens only to have them change their opinions as new circumstances and experiences appear. They will try on different personalities as they move from literal thinking to abstract thinking, and their beliefs or "creeds" will change accordingly.

Teenagers are often passionate about fairness and justice. They can be more sensitive to puppies than to parents. Despite their complaints about having responsibilities like doing homework or practicing the piano, they do enjoy the challenge in doing things well. *"I don't want to do homework, but I appreciate the A grade I got on the test"* or *"I hate soccer practice, but glad we won the game."* While they may begin to assess the variety of points of view surrounding an issue, their emotions often cloud their judgment. Their beliefs or "creeds" motivate how they act or react to life's experiences; they help determine with whom they will or will not associate, and they can cause considerable joy or grief, both for themselves and for others (parents). Teen beliefs are powerful motivators in their future development.

Precisely because teens are "so into" and sensitive about feelings and stating what they believe and what matters to them, suggests that making use of creeds or encouraging creedal thinking as a learning tool for increasing faith formation has great potential. It is to promote the process from being able to state your beliefs regarding one aspect of life to transitioning to doing the same in other aspects. If a student can state and defend beliefs regarding the importance of peer relationships then that same student can potentially transition to stating and defending beliefs about faith practices. It's a matter of immersion in the process of creedal thinking; that practice in the art will lead to proficiency. At a time when the research clearly indicates that teens struggle with expressing a faith and stumble when trying to describe it, creeds can be the very tool to sharpen their focus and serve as a reference point for faith formation and growth. Creedal thinking is that very process that enables young people to practice stating beliefs and defending them.

Witnessing to the truth.

When introducing creedal thinking with teenagers, some basic groundwork needs to be done before creeds can serve as translators and clarifiers' of the beliefs and practices of the faith. Witnessing is a foundation block for creeds.

Creeds are a form of witnessing. The idea of a witness is not a foreign concept to even the youngest of confirmation students. Defined in simple terms, a witness is one who can give a personal account of something seen, heard, or experienced. The witness testifies to the truth as experienced. It may turn out not to be "the truth," but that's not what is important. What is important is to encourage students to tell the truth "as they see it" and not to fear testifying. Testifying is the backbone of a creed. If students are to be encouraged to use creeds for moving "conversational faith," towards "consequential faith" they need first to dissect the meaning of testimony. Here's a simple example for use with confirmations students:

One day John's mother asked him to go to the local Stop and Shop to get a gallon of milk. As he was about to enter the store, he was nearly bowled over by a person exiting. He was in a great hurry.

When John entered the store, the clerk told him he was just robbed by the person leaving. Did John recognize him?

John thought for a moment and then realized, yes he did. It was Bill Williams. Later that afternoon, John was called to the police station to testify to what he saw. The officer asked him, "Are you sure it was Bill Williams?" Bill was arrested.

About a week later, John read in the newspaper that a man named Hank Schneider confessed.

Now ask your students the following:

- Did John tell the truth when he accused Bill of the robbery?
- Just because he was wrong, did he perjure himself? (Intentionally tell a lie)

Ease student's fear of creeds as "a statement of belief" by helping them understand that testifying is a form of perception. It is telling the truth as you perceive it in that place and at that time. If the person is fearful of consequences for stating beliefs that might turn out not to be "the whole truth and nothing but the truth" than working with creeds as a means for enhancing conversational faith becomes more difficult. (*More activities related to witnessing are available in the addendum)*

Teens are very susceptible to the witness of others. When a teen idol, pop star, or sports figures indicates they use a certain product, teens respond to that "witnessing" unequivocally. It behooves the confirmation teacher to seek out and employ as many examples of witnessing as can be garnered. Be as simplistic as possible. Point to advertising as an example of how people respond to witnessing. Suggest and demonstrate how we witness events that are important to us and the ways we find to share the essence of these events with other people. This can be as simple as reminding kids that they like to share with friends what they got for Christmas or why it is important to them to tell their parents when they aced a test. Because they were important events and they witnessed them, they are motivated to share them. The intent is to create an atmosphere in which teens are comfortable with the concept of testimony and witness as ground work for introducing and using creeds.

Basic beliefs - a starting point.

Even though creeds (basic beliefs) are an intuitive part of all people's experience, it is best to assume the ability to state spiritual beliefs as creeds does not come instinctively. Even ordinary, garden variety beliefs are learned and practiced before they are comfortable and acceptable tools for expressing faith practices. Introducing the practice of stating beliefs does not have to be complicated. The confirmation teacher can help students become comfortable using language to state beliefs by incorporating creeds into every day experiences of teenagers.

Introduce a creed

Attempting to introduce the concepts of creedal thinking to a class of adolescent confirmation students can sometimes feel daunting, but not overwhelming I once had a small class of six students for whom I printed out the Apostles Creed.

"Let's read this together," I instructed them. "Then we will see what parts we understand and what parts we struggled with."

We read it together aloud. During the reading, I noticed considerable giggling and some poking of each other.

"What's so funny," I asked.

"We thought you meant the apostles *greed,* and I wondered what they wanted so badly they couldn't have." responded one boy.

"Maybe we could believe all this stuff if we knew what they were talking about," a second student chimed in. "It sounds like foreign language. What does it have to do with God and church and stuff like that?"

"Are we supposed to buy into this stuff? It's got nothing to do with my life" I'm into sports and friends and doing things with my family. I believe in God like my parents do, but it's much simpler than this," another student piped in.

"Okay. Fair enough," I responded. "Let's try it a different way. You know what *is* important to you, so let's talk about that. Robin, can you tell us, the whole class, what is most important to you about your friends?"

"Yeah," she said. "I like doing things with my friends. We talk about stuff that I can't talk to my parents about. Sometimes we get mad at each other, but then we make up. My best friend is my best friend because we like to do the same things."

"That's a creed," I told her.

"A what?"

"A creed. A statement of what you believe. You told us what is important to you right now and why it's important. That's what creeds do."

We then followed this exercise by asking each student to write down what they believed was important to them about friends, about family, and about education. They were extremely articulate.

"You say your friends are important, but friends are usually the first to tell lies about you," I told them. "And your families just get in the way of your doing what you want." I had hit a sore point and it generated some lively responses.

"Then they are not really your friends," was the response agreed upon by the group. "Friends don't tell lies. If they do, you need to find new friends. But it's always good to have friends that support you." They surprised me with the intensity of their defense of friends.

"Yeah, families can sometimes be a pain in the you know what," one kid replied with a bit of sarcasm in his voice. "But I depend on them even though I don't always agree with what they want me to do."

I acted as a devil's advocate, attempting to point out flaws in each of their responses to beliefs about friends, family and education. It helped them see that their statements of beliefs, were not really beliefs unless they were willing to defend them. The real statements of strong beliefs came mostly after they were challenged.

As a tool for articulating one's practice of faith encourage confirmands to state what they believe about almost any topic important to them. Consider such topics as the myth of independence, their responses to advertising, pop culture, the influence of teen pop stars, their perception of the importance of body image, school tests as indicators of smartness, romantic relationships, or sleep. Teens spend an inordinate amount of time and energy cogitating and being overly anxious about these issues. Once introduced, adolescents can be extremely articulate when discussing these. When you question them about defending their beliefs, they can become down right agitated and forthright. The point is, if you expect teens to comprehend the concept of creeds as statements of belief then practice with belief statements in appropriately important areas of their lives is a prerequisite.

The objective of all these exercises is to promote dialogue with adolescents about what they believe, get them to talk with you and with each other about issues of importance and show a willingness to defend and support what they believe. It is not a difficult transition to move from dialogue about matters of interest to teens to dialogue about faith practices. The process is the same, only the content is different.

I next wrote the following on some newsprint *"Faith is..."* and asked them each to complete the sentence. From their previous exposure and practice making and defending strongly held beliefs, they tackled this activity with great enthusiasm. Again, even though their statements were rudimentary, when challenged, they defended them.

Remember, your task is to use creedal thinking as a means for dialogue about faith beliefs and faith practices. The more you engage the student in dialogue, the more practice the student has in articulating issues of faith.

Growth in faith.

There are other issues that also demand teachers' attention. If creeds are to become avenues for students to express and grow their practices of faith, kids will benefit by knowing how beliefs change over time due to new circumstances. I used the following dialogue to illustrate this:

"How many of you still believe in Santa Claus?" I asked my confirmation class.

A few hands went up, and the rest of the class stared at them.

"What? What's the problem?" these few exclaimed as they looked around to gauge the response of the rest of the group. Clearly they were just attempting to stand out by being different. They expounded on the benefits of believing, (maybe you won't get any presents if you don't believe) but eventually admitted they didn't really believe Santa existed. My impression was they felt it a matter of maturing to give up on Santa.

Now it's time for a reality check and a chance to infuse some theological education into the minds of adolescents. Begin a dialogue about Santa Claus. With few exceptions, teen's denial of Santa Claus is one of the first proclamations they make to prove their maturity. Maybe yes, maybe no. So I asked them, "When you were younger, what did you believe about Santa Clause?"

"He wore a red suit, had a long beard, and was very nice to good children and not so nice to bad kids. He came down the chimney on Christmas Eve, and left presents," were a few notable remembrances.

"So when you think about Santa Claus now, what are your beliefs, if you have any?" I asked.

"I guess he's still around, but I think about him differently. I want him to symbolize the spirit of Christmas, you know, the gift giving and all that." That summarized most of the kid's responses.

"So you still believe in Santa Claus only differently now." I pointed out how our beliefs may change as we grow older, but the concept of Santa remains the same. I then suggested the same thing might be true about our beliefs in God.

I asked the class to take a sheet of paper, draw a line from top to bottom down the middle. On the top left side write "used to thinks". On the top right side write, "now I thinks."

Some further instructions. "Below the first column, use words or phrases that you used to think about God when you were young. In the next column, write down words or phrases you think about God now."

They did this. The results were particularly revealing. In the" used to thinks" column they used words like old man with a beard, lived in heaven, and watched when you sneaked a smoke behind the barn. In the "now I thinks" column, they disclosed phrases such as God loves everyone, God is spirit, God is everywhere, and God cares about people. The two lists clearly showed differing perspectives about God. When left to their own devices, teens can grasp that beliefs can change. People grow more perceptive and express what's true about matters differently at different ages and stages without having to abandon basic beliefs. Once kids recognize this for themselves, they become more open to an evolving faith, a faith that grows. Faith issues are best expressed in words that reflect present perceptions. You are now on your way to utilizing creedal thinking in a creative and functional way.

Invariably the words used to describe God as a child will reflect a concrete and simplistic understanding of God while the words or phrases used to describe God now will incorporate abstract concepts and symbols. Help students recognize that God doesn't change, but our perceptions of God change. The statements we use to describe our beliefs reflect our changing perceptions. Such a revelation helps students to articulate their beliefs about God. It invites them into dialogue about faith beliefs and practices, the basics of creedal thinking. Dialogue about God that emerges from creedal thinking accepts that truth may be relative (a kind of truth for me and truth for you) but at the same time challenges the students to consider other viewpoints and perspectives and to defend positions.

Recognizing when they cannot defend beliefs is a beginning point for growing in faith beliefs. Confirmation, as an educational setting, is an exceptional opportunity to engage kids with conversational faith; a setting in which we might utilize the best methods of dialogue as a tool for increasing faith awareness and faith nurture.

5

DOES EVERYTHING HAVE A PURPOSE?

"If you don't know where you're going, you'll end up someplace else."

"In the beginning, God Created the earth, and he
looked upon it in His cosmic loneliness.
And Gods said, 'Let us
make living creatures out of mud, so the mud can see
what we have done.' And God created
every living creature that moves.
Mud as man sat up, looked around, and spoke.
Man blinked. 'What's the purpose of all this,' he asked politely.
'Everything must have a purpose?' asked God.
'Certainly,' said man.
'Then I leave it to you to think of one for all of this," said God.
And he went away."

--*Cat's Cradle,* Kurt Vonnegut

We are a purpose driven people, no doubt about that. We don't like doing anything unless it has a purpose. Without purpose, not only would life feel meaningless and we would wander aimlessly, but we also might even sink into utter chaos. So...everything must have a purpose.

Recent research questions the effectiveness of our efforts toward forming a "consequential" faith for teenagers. Data suggests it might be a huge waste of time. I believe part of the problem lies with our inability focus on clear objectives. We evolve vague and ambiguous purposes statements. We don't know what we want to achieve.

Deciding on an end product or purpose for educating teenagers' about religion may be the hardest task we have to do, but also among the most imperative. Planning is the key to effective education, we already know that. All good planning begins by knowing where we want to go before embarking on the mission. Be clear about a purpose. Evidence suggests, however, that we don't really know where we are headed or where we want our kids to be as we seek to create a faith in adolescents.

Not all purposes are of equal value. We define purpose differently for differing aspects of our life. We evolve a purpose for our work, for our families, for our recreation, even for our relationships. Purposes differ, but the definition of purpose remains the same. Dictionaries define purpose as follows:

- Something one intends to do.
- Acting by design.
- Planning with a specific end in view.

Sounds simple enough. We don't spend a large amount of time thinking about what purposes we have in life. We don't need to. Purpose is a simple matter, something we do for ourselves (and for others) almost without thinking.

Here's a simple definition:

> *"Purpose statements are declarative sentences which summarize proposed actions and goals."*
>
> (*Finding Purpose with a Purpose Statement*, by Ken Maschke, Leadership Magazine, V. 12, Oct., 2103.)

So...hardly an action, an event, or a moment of our life is without purpose. Can you imagine getting up each morning without a clue as to how you are going to spend the day? Sounds like what retirement ought to be, the dream of the working stiff having nothing to do all day. Even if you have not written down the purposes you what to accomplish this day, unconsciously you still have a purpose. Even the retired have a purpose - to do what they please or nothing at all if that's what pleases them. Without purpose we live lives of extreme ambiguity, never knowing if we are making forward progress or losing ground. Mostly we remain in limbo when purposes elude us.

A purpose is intentional.

Purposes need to be explicit. They need to state unequivocally what you intend to happen. Fuzzy, non-specific purposes confuse rather than clarify. They hold out unrealistic hopes and unrealized dreams because our purpose or goal is vague. In our haste, we don't take the time to make clear goals. Without a clear purpose or an achievable goal we are like a sailboat that has lost its rudder, at the mercy of the shifting wind.

Purpose vs. goals.

The terms "purpose" and "goal "are different, but are often used interchangeably. The wordsmiths among us might make a case for using one or the other to avoid confusion, but for the rest of us, the difference is too slight to worry about. When examining purpose statements for confirmation programs, churches tend to use the two terms interchangeably.

When purpose and goal are interlinked it makes it difficult to differentiate between the two. One of the differences between them is the time factor. People try to reach goals by setting time lines or deadlines. A purpose does not have a deadline, it is rather a vision of the future; a direction to go.

We define a goal as the point one wishes to achieve. A purpose is defined by the reason why one hopes to achieve a goal. A goal is always going forward; a purpose has no movement. We measure a goal's progress. We cannot measure a purpose. A goal has a specific target; a purpose does not. A goal has a bulls eye, a vision is without a target.

Let's take a simple example. You find that your life has become too stressed. You can't continue to live with this level of apprehension and anxiety. You imagine that a vacation will help dissolve the stress and lower your anxiety levels. First of all you need to determine a purpose; your purpose is to learn to relax. Your goal is to take a vacation. A vacation will help your achieve your purpose of relaxation. Goals are means for achieving your purpose; your purpose is to relieve stress; your goal is to accomplish a vacation. If the vacation does not relieve your stress, than it is not a means to accomplish your purpose. Be careful what you chose as the medium for achieving your goals. Don't confuse the means to accomplish a goal (take a vacation) with the purpose of the vacation (relieve stress). Otherwise, your intended purpose becomes unrealized.

Having a purpose points us toward an end, an objective, some reason for our actions or goals. Purpose statements, as reiterated earlier, need to be specific. The following are guidelines for making an effective purpose statement:

- It is precise. It describes with exactness what you intend.
- It is concise. Too much wording tends to confuse
- It is clear. It means what it says and says what it means
- It is not a goal, but it is a statement that points toward a conclusion, an achievable end, or a specific direction

Back to our example. If the purpose of a vacation is to relieve stress, plans will be made to guarantee a very relaxing vacation; a time to relieve all stress and completely unwind. Once that's accomplished then the vacation (the goal) qualifies as a means for achieving the purpose (relaxation).

I share this brief analysis of purposes because I feel strongly that confusion reigns with religious instructors. For centuries educators have addressed the necessity of preparing children to achieve a mature adult faith with great enthusiasm. Although there has been general agreement regarding the need for this transitional education, particularly in the faith communities, the means to the end remains vague and imprecise.

Confirmation, as a process of faith formation with adolescents, suffers from a variety of ambiguous purposes statements. Most purpose statements I have come across sound admirable, but unfortunately remain vague, imprecise, and overly generalized. They tend to confuse rather than clarify. Confirmation needs to be subjected to the same scrutiny about its purpose, perhaps even more so, than that given to any other educational venture. The effectiveness of confirmation is too important to rely on fuzzy, non-specific purpose statements.

The consequences of faulty purpose statements are fatal. Fuzzy, non-specific statements render confirmation education unproductive and unworkable. They lack progress toward specific goals. Perhaps more than any other circumstance, the failure to thoroughly think through the purpose for which confirmation education is intended is the primary, if not the only reason, why confirmation does not achieve effective results. That's a pretty pungent statement and needs some documentation to support it. So let's look at a few purpose statements from congregations around the country.

Dr. William Willimon, acting as a consultant to his local church, once remarked about his goals for the confirmation program, *"All I want," he said, "is a group of youth who may one day grow up to resemble John Black."*(*Taking Confirmation Out of the Classroom*, Christian Century, March 16, 1988, p 271 used by permission). Dr. Willimon must have known and greatly admired John Black. He saw him as an esteemed Christian, reflecting all the qualities that he thought essential for a good Christian. If each confirmation student were to end up like John Black, the program achieved its purpose. Can't get more specific than this. The only remaining task is to engineer a program that achieves this result.

One of Dr. Willimon's associates wishing to continue the conversation responded with the following observation. *"One can't devise appropriate educational methods until one has first defined what it is that one wants to teach. What is the end product of the confirmation? What do we hope to accomplish"* (Ibid, p271 used by permission). The crux of the problem; decide first on a purpose, the end product; a statement that is precise, concise, and points toward an achievable conclusion.

Then set your goals towards achieving the purpose. Here is where most purposes statements for confirmation fail. They become ambiguous and abstruse and without measurable goals. The educator has no way to determine success, other than a hunch.

Please note that it is the latter part of the above statement that matters, the part about what is hoped to be accomplish; the former part, the part of about deciding what one wants to teach, does not add clarity. Most of the statements we will examine falter on this very point; they are teacher centered, rather than student centered. They indicate what the teacher will do rather than what the student will learn. Any educational objective worth its salt sets its priority on what the student will learn, not what the teacher will teach. (*As a result of my teaching, the student will learn…).*Too many times what the teacher intends is not what the student learns.

In one set of curriculum for confirmation education of the Presbyterian Church (USA), the stated purpose is, "*For youth, ages twelve and older to understand their baptism, their faith commitment, and their place in the church.*" (We Believe: God's Word for God's People, p3). Sounds like it is student centered, but the content of the courses, the individual sessions are all about what the teacher will do. The leader will…is a constant theme, not "the student will". Despite the student activities to accompany what the teacher teaches, the sessions remain teacher centered.

St Paul Lutheran Church issues the following as its purpose statement:

> *"Confirmation is a pastoral and educational ministry of the church, which helps families to help their baptized children… to identify more deeply with the Christian community and participate more fully in its mission.".*

"Identifying more deeply" and "participating more fully" are indeterminate and largely ambiguous statements. They don't contribute significantly towards achieving an end result. "More deeply" and "participate more fully" are certainly not precise about what the student will accomplish. "More" is too imprecise. They describe what the teacher would like to teach, not what the student will learn. Both are subjective to the point of being abstruse.

Let's look at one more purpose statement. This one comes from the Lewinsville Presbyterian Church:

> *"The purpose of confirmation is to provide an opportunity to explore the meaning of the Christian faith as understood in the Presbyterian tradition. Students are asked to struggle with all this means for them personally."*

"Exploring" and "struggling" are worthwhile endeavors but remain ambiguous. Each can be interpreted differently by different people. They do not make for a precise purpose or a specific goal that one can evaluate to determine if success is achieved.

When perusing a whole host of purpose statements of local congregations, a plethora of statements emerge. Common denominators appear; similar words and phrases that are less than revealing of any specific purpose. Phrases such as faith formation, exploring, discovering, experiencing, and struggling are among a few of the many catch words. These key words imply that confirmation is a process, an exercise that each student must endure; certainly a worthwhile endeavor, but without a specific end in mind. They make it sound exciting, gripping, invigorating, and action-packed. One congregation in the Northeast defines the purpose of confirmation as a "faith exploration process". Adolescents most likely are in awe of exploration, but they expect to find something concrete at the end of the search. Most of these words and phrases imply a journey; that the confirmands will be going somewhere, but where they will end up remains unspecified. It's a journey without a destination. As an afterthought, the same church cited above lists as part of its purpose, "attendance is an absolute requirement but can be negotiated." So much for clarity of purpose.

Teacher centered or student centered.

If the purpose of confirmation education is the end product, a faith that is formed, then the question of whether the purpose statement is teacher centered or student centered matters greatly. Teacher centered goals are much easier to define. They are what the teacher intends to do. *"I will teach my students what the bible says about Jesus"* or *"I will teach the Ten Commandments."* All are teacher centered. They inform what the teacher will teach, but say nothing about what the students will learn. These two functions can be radically different. Here is where purpose and goal differentiate. Teacher centered purposes meet the criteria of "something one intends to do, but does not point toward a conclusion; a specific end." What the student learns can be radically different from what the teacher intends that the student learn.

I propose an example that illustrates this point precisely. A mother is experiencing the problem of her young daughter running out into a busy street chasing a wayward ball. The mother has repeatedly lectured the girl about the dangers of traffic in the street. One day she witnesses the girl chasing a loose ball into the street. Mom can't stand the anxiety anymore and gives the girl a whack across the backside out of frustration. Question: what has the little girl learned?

The intent of Mom was to keep her out of the street. The little girl may never do this again, but she also learns that might-makes-right; that violence produces results. Perhaps she learns to hit others as a way to get her way. An extreme example; perhaps so, but it also demonstrates that what the teacher intends is not always what the student learns.

Student centered purposes and goals mandate that the teacher consider first and foremost what the student will learn and precisely how the student will change. Considerer the end product. I don't mean to sound like I think people are commodities, but the concept of end product best describes what we want to have happen to the student as a result of what we do for the student. Purpose statements for confirmation, of necessity, must be clear about how each student will emulate Mr. Black.

Vision and purpose statements.

Although purpose statements contain visions, there is a slight difference between a vision and a purpose. Many congregations spend long hours in committee deciding upon a "vision" for the parishioners. A vision, loosely defined, is a view towards the future. It is a long range perspective describing a hoped-for outcome. It is like looking through binoculars at a faraway place wishing you were there. The local congregation might describe its vision as "to create a world in which the good news of God's kingdom is evident and expressed." Such a statement might go on to amend the vision with tactics used to achieve the vision. Phrases like "equipping the saints for ministry," or "to love and care for one another as God's people," inspire the congregation to work towards the vision. These do not contain specifics enough to qualify as a purpose or goal, only a vision toward which one wants to head.

A purpose, by necessity, needs to be specific. It carries with it goals as specific steps toward achieving the purpose. If it remains ambiguous, any steps toward reaching the goal flounder with obscurity. The goal is like the object seen through the binoculars.

A confirmation map.

Confirmation as a tool for forming a faith for adolescents is, first and foremost, an educational venture. Despite the feeling that "religious" thoughts are ethereal and not dependent upon rational modes of thinking, confirmation is an educational journey and subject to the best methods of educational teaching. It is dependent upon establishing clear goals and objectives for the learners. Those who teach as well as those who are learning need a "map" that shows how a purpose (or goal) is achieved.

Unfortunately, religion teachers too often fail to be precise and clear in their purposes. We think that Christian education stands apart from secular education. It is spiritual in nature and does not require us to be specific. We worry that by being specific we lose some of the ethereal nature of religious thinking.

Purpose statements about faith formation require strong and clear language; more than hoping or wishing. Although goals differ from purposes, the variance is slight. For purposes to be meaningful, they need to meet the following criteria

Purposes must be specific: Remember Mr. Black. He was the man that Reverend William Willimon wanted his confirmation students to emulate. That's a specific goal or purpose. Confirmation purposes may not always seek out clones of real people like Mr. Black, but they must state what is to be accomplished as a result of the confirmation process.

Purposes are measureable. Has the student learned what was expected? There can be both objective and subjective tests to measure faith formation purposes. Although not as specific as goals, purposes still need a sense of being able to be completed. Objectively, you can test if the students have knowledge of the bible, of the tenets of the Christian faith, or requirements of membership in the church. Just ask them. If they give the right answers, you can measure their success.

Subjective measurement of one's faith is more difficult to determine. Dialogue with the student built around questions pertaining to the meaning of the student's religious beliefs and practices can be very revealing of the strength or weakness of that faith. Here is where the use of creeds and creedal thinking can become extremely helpful.

Purposes are attainable. Simply put, your choice of purpose for the teenager's faith formation must be reasonable, age appropriate, and easily recognized. Because adults and teens have different levels of spiritual comprehension, take care when defining the purpose. As adults we are comfortable with abstract language and religious symbolism. Teenagers have not yet mastered the full scope of conceptual thinking. Teenagers will fail to grasp faith formation when the language is incomprehensible to them.

Language confusion is a constant problem for adolescents attempting to articulate their faith. Let this story illustrate. A young child went to visit her grandmother in the hospital.

She was recovering from open heart surgery. When she arrived, her grandmother told her, hoping to relieve the child of any anxiety, "my heart is almost good as new. The doctors went inside me and fixed it right up."

The child looked puzzled, and then responded, "Grandma, did they see God in there?"

Once, when she was younger, she asked her church school teacher where God lived.

Her teacher replied, "In your heart, my dear, in your heart."

It is confusing for young people to make the transition from concrete thinking to abstract concepts. It can be counterproductive when adults use abstract concepts when describing spiritual matters among children. Experience has shown that children learn best when moving from familiar experiences to unfamiliar ones. For the teenager struggling with religious beliefs, it is helpful to affirm what they presently believe and then coax them slowly toward a more mature belief.

If you have the task of creating a purpose statement for confirmation, the following characteristic are helpful in clarifying your goals (1) Begin each purpose or goal statement with the word "to." (2) Follow with an action word. (3) Identify what is to be accomplished. (4) Identify how it is to be accomplished. (5) Set target dates. (6) Specify what and when, not how or why. Follow these criteria and you are less likely to be burdened by what you hope the student will learn and what, in fact, the student actually does learn.

Quality management.

Recently I read an article in a trade magazine that captured my attention. The subject was "quality management." Not a subject about which I have any measure of expertise. But it struck me that what the author was referring to had broad application to teaching teenagers about faith. Just the title - quality management – I am sure raises the hackles of religious educators. They want to deal with the ethereal, not the practical. But the idea struck me that this concept was particularly apt for educational theory. The heart of quality management maintains that if you want a good product to emanate from your system, management has to test the system continually and make adjustments. If they don't, they'll turn out bad parts more often than good parts.

Evaluation is the key to quality management. Two forms of evaluation are necessary. 1. The ability to test the administrators – teachers, planners, course designers – and all others who orchestrate the learning process and environment. 2. The ability to test the student's cognitive understanding of the course content. The two tests intermingle, that is to say, the test of the student's comprehension is as much a test of the administrators ability. If a student cannot comprehend what is being taught, the fault is likely to reside with the administrator's ability to design and present.

In religious education, we have gotten out of the habit of demanding accountability by both administrators and students. Accountability often requires that certain content be remembered. Hardly a discipline exists – athletics, dance, math, music, medicine – where demands are not made that practitioners remember stuff. Students in these disciplines are held accountable for remembering what they have learned; they are tested frequently.

Not so with faith content or religious practices. Religious educator's distain memorization. Testing is not in the cards. Testing is demeaning, unnecessary, and without merit or value. Unfortunately where we demand little, little is expected. We refuse to hold either administrators or students accountable and responsible for what they are supposed to know. It's a scandal to confirm students who go through the motions but for whom there is no inkling of their level of understanding because we refuse to test them. The need for accountability in religious education is reflected in the words of David Armstrong when he states, *"It is no less sensible to demand appropriate religious knowledge than for anything else. To not do this presupposes that religious matters are somehow only private, or unimportant, or optional, or separated from the mind and common sense."* (David Armstrong, *Biblical Evidence for Catholicism*: Dave's Topical Bible, Sophia Institute Press, *2009*)

Faith formation and community.

The nature of the religious experience for both adults and teens does not completely lie in the objective realm. Much of this experience is personal and subjective. Those congregations advocating for the experiential side of faith formation have a more difficult time forming purpose statements. The "experiential" realm of teenage faith formation resides in building community as a place of support and experiencing the deeper sense of belonging to the Christian community. This process of building relationships expands well beyond knowing the basic tenets of Christianity. To achieve this aspect of faith formation, more emphasis is placed on mentor experiences; connecting with other Christians, and building on these relationships.

6

CHRISTIANS UNDER CONSTRUCTION

"The good news about confirmation ministry is that there is no one right way to do it. The major challenge of confirmation ministry is...there is no one right way to do it."

---*Reframing Confirmation* by Kathy Christenson

There is always something disturbing and troublesome when considering the circumstances of teenagers. What's troubling the faith formation of teens is and will probably always be a challenge. But hope remains. Despite the challenge, the good news is that teenagers have a vivid imagination and insatiable curiosity. This works in their favor. I propose that this imagination and curiosity will eventually win out. It will become a motivator and source for faith formation, but it will need considerable nurturing along the way.

Perhaps one of the best tools we have for nurturing a *"consequential"* faith for teenagers is to engage them in dialogue. Talking *with*, not *at* teens, emboldens their curiosity, and encourages their self-discovery. Don't be afraid of their doubts and reservations about what they believe or don't believe about religion and faith practices. It's natural for them to be suspicious and sometimes even outlandish in their beliefs. Teenagers can be scary, but you are the adult.

Having a conversation and providing active listening encourages adolescent's willingness to share attitudes and opinions unencumbered. What you will learn by just paying attention and listening to teens will amaze you.

Intelligence, combined with resourcefulness and a spirit of inquiry have to be among the most compelling of attributes bestowed on humans by the creator God. They are what distinguishes us from the "lower forms" and contribute significantly to the human endeavor to seek after God. At the root of our curiosity lies an insatiable imagination, a sense of wonderment and amazement about the world in which we live. I can only imagine that this must be how God willed it. God must thoroughly enjoy watching humans discover their spirituality and expand their awe and wonder over the mystery of God.

I hope you agree with the previous paragraph. It makes sense and has credence for you as a mature Christian. It is part of your mantra. But try to convince a 14 year old teenager that he also has "an insatiable imagination and curiosity" about God and you will probably meet with fierce resistance. "No I don't," he will probably respond. But don't give up. The truth is that your teen does have this imagination and will eventually be, at the very least, curious about the mystery of God.

We all live on the threshold between independence and dependence, particularly during the adolescent years. When teens do think about religion, they seem to vacillate between being for and against God or they want to limit God's input into their lives. Both teens and adults are constantly crossing back and forth between a complete obedience to God and a continual questioning of God's very existence. We don't want God to be too close, but not too far away either.

There are those times when we adamantly maintain our self-sufficiency, living fully without aid or reliance or trust in God. We think we can go it alone. We choose not to live with God, if not altogether ignoring God. We behave badly as Christians. We figure we can't live with a God who demands obedience and sustaining dependence when what we really want is to be independent and self-sufficient. The two appear incompatible. Therein lays the dilemma for teenagers, caught in the middle. It is always a struggle for the teen between emerging independence of an individual and the stable safe dependence of societal and family support.

And then there are those times when we freely and willingly acquiesce to God. We acknowledge that we live and breathe and have our being solely by the grace of God. We know we are wholly dependent upon God's providence. We can't function fully without God. We seem to want it both ways. The 14 year old teenager already experiences this dichotomy by virtue of his acquiescence to the religion of his parents while at the same time declaring his emerging independence. This is as much a problem for the secure and mature Christian adult as it is for the teenager.

Divine headache.

We probably cause God great heartburn and severe headaches as we constantly move between these two extremes – for God and ignore God. But I suspect that God has grown used to this. Relationships are never free from complications, whether human or divine. But like all healthy relationships, the God/human relationship thrives only when mutual examination, independent respect, and a large dose of tolerance and patience is present. We strive to unravel the mysteries of God. We want to know more about God. We are not (or shouldn't be) satisfied that God remains a mystery. Our search for the divine in our life seems always to be more than merely a faith that is "*...the assurance of things hoped for, the conviction of things not seen*" (Hebrews11:1 RSV).

Despite that "by faith" humans have evolved a sustaining relationship with God; we continue to want to struggle with the meaning and implications of that faith. Perhaps it is at this very point of our continual search for meaning in that relationship that our curiosity is most vivid. Our insatiable curiosity about matters of the spirit often fetches big dividends. God seems willing to reveal more and more of God's mystery to us the more we enquire.

When we know that we know.

I'm a struggling Christian just as any teenager might be. I am still learning and haven't yet arrived. I would like to complete my Christian journey, but I know that it is a life-time pursuit. I am still becoming a Christian and I can live with that. This attitude is one that I like to have pass on to adolescents; that they don't need to declare their Christianity; they need only to be willing to grow into it. Once given permission to be partly religious without a complete emersion allows teenagers to relax and be more open to new spiritual ideas.

Every once in a while, however, I come across some Christians who are sure they are completely Christian, fully Christian, and "know that they know" all there is to know about being Christian. These are people, sometimes even your good friends, so completely convinced that they know what God wants, so assured that they are right about faithfulness, and so resolved that their thoughts and actions are full of righteousness, that they no longer even need think about it. Their Christian faith springs spontaneously. They "know that they know." They want to know why I don't know what they know.

I don't always have an answer for them. To confront such a person so convinced and so entrenched in their parochial perspective is to experience a faith that has become an enigma, if not a paradox. Intimidation does little toward forming faith. Religious bullying serves to further alienate teens from embracing religion.

One MSNBC commentator, Michael Ventra (msnbc.com, Friday, January 21, 2005) became visibly upset with certain "know it all Christians" who claim infallibility on all things religious and cultural. Ventra labeled them as *"crackpot Christians…fools of all persuasions who have perverted religious text for their own selfish purposes."* He further asserted that *"these crackpot Christians have succeeded in doing something I thought would be impossible: they're giving Jesus Christ a bad name."* Ventra is a bit extreme in his criticism, but does successfully raise the issue of religious paranoia.

To hint of doubt by those "who know that they know" is an affront to their faith. If, they reason, the essence of faith is about having complete "*...assurance of things hoped for, the conviction of things not seen*" (Hebrews 11:1 RSV) then to dare to question Holy Scriptures is an anathema. How can the inspired word of God be doubted? It is not to be questioned. It is not to be analyzed or examined or even evaluated. Dissection or diagnosis of any sort is unthinkable and unacceptable.

But such an attitude of entrenchment is an obstacle to growth in faith. It stymies the ability of God to "break forth," to fully and mysteriously reveal himself to us. I only wish these folks knew what they were missing. Teenagers are easily tempted by this attitude. They often feel that once they say they "know" Jesus, then they no longer need be open to discussion and can move on to other matters. In fact, what we hope for our teens is not that they just know *about* Jesus, but that they know what Jesus *is about*.

In the past few decades, as much as in any other period of history, it has been the power of people's religious beliefs that has ushered in drastic changes in our world. Some good, some not so good. The change, however, has little to do with a change in beliefs but rather a change in attitudes and perspectives informed by those beliefs. They take on political and economic importance. Entrenched religious viewpoints are as often the root causes for violence as they are for peace. Entrenched and unyielding religious beliefs affect not only our personal relationships, but our political, cultural and educational perspectives as well.

Faith under examination.

A life that is unexamined is not worth living, a thought expressed by the thinker Socrates four hundred years before Christ that rings as true in the arena of religious thought and spiritual development as it does in any known human inquiry. There can be no circumstances that can justify not examining the impact and implications of God's Word for our time and in our place. There should be nothing that impedes our curiosity about the mysterious realm of God. Without the motivation for examining our spiritual foundations there can be no growth in our understanding of God and consequently no growth in our faithfulness toward God. Faith is not formed from ignorance.

"When I look at thy heavens, the
work of thy fingers,
The moon and the stars which thou hast established;
what is man that thou art
mindful of him,
and the son of man that thou dost care for him?

Yet thou hast made him little
less than God,
and dost crowned them with glory and honor."
(Psalm 8:3-5).

To show how much God cares for us, God has given each of us a vivid imagination and an insatiable curiosity. These have the highest priority among the "glory and honor" that God dost crown us with. To confess that God might have made us "little lower than God" is a good starting point to begin our growth in faith. It acknowledges that we are not exactly like God, not even close to being God, but live in a unique relationship with God. It's almost as if God is challenging us in that relationship; we are dared to seek to know as much about God as is possible despite that we are merely human. "*Go ahead,*" God seems to be saying, "*use your imagination and curiosity I have given you to try to unravel the mystery of God.*"

Throughout scriptures, we are constantly bombarded with the "enquiring mind" of the biblical writers. They seem concerned with not only what might be on the mind of God, but also with what difference knowing about God might make in our lives. They show great concern for the question of how does knowing about God affect who they are and how they are going to act in their own time and place. The patriarchs of the faith have no qualms about their self-doubt and their need to inquire about God. Their intuitiveness never seems to irritate God; it only challenges God to more eagerly intervene in the realm of humans. Such a narratives speak to the building of a comprehensive relationship between God and God's people, and like any relationship, builds upon the trust and responsiveness of each other. God is not intimidated by our searching. God welcomes it.

Our inquisitiveness does not threaten God. Take Psalm 8 for instance. Clearly the writer is struggling with the implications of faith in God when the question is raised, "*What are human beings that you are mindful of them?*" The writer is wondering about the unique place of humankind in God's scheme of things. He isn't sure. He doesn't sound overly confident. He wants to know the implications of made "in the likeness of God." He is struggling not only with why God would care about him but also what difference that might make in his life. He doesn't have an answer any more than he can claim to know what God looks like. He is forming a faith. He knows it's not complete and may never be complete but his constant scrutiny keeps his faith vibrant. Does the inquisitiveness of this writer threaten God? Not hardly. The writer is merely examining the core theological conviction between God and God's people.

Intuitiveness and challenge are at the heart of teenage curiosity. Teens thrive on questioning the status quo. Like the man who questions why God would care about him, teens will examine the same attitudes; why would my parents, my friends, even God care about me?

At the very beginning (Genesis 1), we are exposed to Adam and Eve's questioning of God's exclusive knowledge of good and evil. Despite its origin as "sin", it proves to be a clue to understanding the kind of relationship established between God and humans; a relationship of both obedience and suspicion. Nothing much has changed over the centuries. Self-centeredness and pride still act as a barrier separating humans from God.

Abraham meets God's quest of a covenant in which he is promised a land, descendants, and a great blessing, with insistent questioning and suspicion. "*But... how am I to know?*" Abraham inquires (Genesis 15:7-8 RSV). Doesn't sound like the unfailing adoration of a man free of uncertainties about God.

It is the same with Moses. Even though "ordained" by God to lead his people, Moses seems consumed by his own feelings of inadequacy. Does he doubt his personal qualifications, yes, and this doubt is tempered by his uncertainty that he has actually encountered the one and only true God. Moses appears consumed by his need for assurance and clarity. He wants to know what this God requires of him. *"But behold, they will not believe me or listen to my voice for they will say, the Lord did not appear to you."* (Exodus 4:1 RSV). In other words, when God says, *"I am who I am"*, Moses wants to know how do I know who you say you are? How do I know what you want? Moses, although unsure of who God is, is never uneasy or embarrassed about expressing his need for reassurance. By expressing his doubt, Moses exposes his own need to examine the implications for this growing relationship.

As much as the Psalmists heap praise on God, equally do they examine and question the ways of the Lord. *"Such knowledge is too wonderful for me; it is high, I cannot attain it… Search me, O God and know my heart"* (Psalm 139:6, 23 RSV). What appears as blind adherence to God's ways is really a wonderment and sense of awe at why God is as God is. Certainly the words expressed cannot be interpreted that the writer knows all about God, or that God is without mystery. Although there is a sense of compliance that God is beyond comprehension, there still exists a hint of suspicion as the writer seeks to understand God.

In the New Testament, the ministry of Jesus may be set in a different locus but there remains an atmosphere of inquiry about ways by which one relates to God. Jesus doesn't assume that all people will know everything about God. His method of teaching about God is often confrontational and elusive. Rarely does Jesus lecture. He does not offer answers nearly as often as he poses questions. He challenges the hearer to search for implications in our relationship with God. He implores people to think hard, to consider and examine diligently the way they relate to God, to each other, and to the world. Obedience to God is required, but God's ways, according to Jesus, are always open to examination.

Attitudes are like habits. Once acquired, they stay with us even when we wish they wouldn't. Much of what Jesus is about has to do with our attitudes. How we feel in our hearts has much to do with how we will act in our lives.

Since so much of what Jesus is about has to do with making and maintaining relationships, both with God and with each other, changing our attitudes about relationships is central to many of the teachings of Jesus. Many of the parables of Jesus are stories about people in particular circumstances that reflect the relationship between people and God as well as between individuals – forgiveness, acceptance, tolerance, altruism. Most often the parable introduces the hearer to the possibility of change modeled after the relationship that is possible with God. Just as Jesus preaches forgiveness from God, so also does he preach forgiveness between people. Jesus' parables require that we examine our attitudes in this light. For instance, in the parable of the Prodigal Son (Luke 15: 11-32), Jesus relates a story about a strained relationship between and father and his two sons. What transpires says much about our attitudes toward forgiveness and how difficult it is for us to change these attitudes. Only by enquiring about the difference this story makes in our lives do we learn about the power of forgiveness.

In the parable of the Good Samaritan (Luke 10: 29-37) we are challenged to examine our attitudes about "neighborliness." We are in the habit of extending generosity to the people we already know and like, but Jesus challenges us to ask, "how to be neighborly, rather than "who is my neighbor;" how we can act generously regardless of who is in need. In the parable of the Rich Fool (Luke 12: 13-21) once again Jesus uses the concept of relationship to encourage us to re-examine the difference between the material and the ethereal.

The teachings of Jesus are always contextual. This means that concepts such as forgiveness, community, human rights, justice, acceptance, power, and reconciliation remain elusive concepts and without meaning or significance until they are inserted into a specific context in our lives. The context, the package around which we wrap our real experiences, provides times and places and circumstances in which we can draw meaning from the teachings of Jesus as they relate to that context.

In the Prodigal Son Parable, the concept is one of forgiveness. Forgiveness makes sense to us only as we consider a context in which we need forgiveness in our lives. Likewise, when considering the parable of the Good Samaritan, the concept is generosity. We make sense of Jesus' teaching when we consider a specific time in our lives when we acted charitably and unconditionally or failed to act generously. A real life context is important to the teens. This context provides the teenager with a connection between what happens to him in real life and what his religion teaches about the circumstance that Jesus encounters.

It is an inherent part of our spiritual development, encouraged by the teachings of Jesus, to weigh the consequences of beliefs and practices, to investigate the implications, to consider the context, and to continually question the ways of God. For instance, when teaching us about how we relate to God, Jesus points us in the direction of how we relate to each other. *"…as you did it to one of the least of these my brethren, you did it to me"* (Matthew 25: 40 RSV). "Now," Jesus appears to imply, "think for yourself what that might mean in your own time and place and circumstances." Clearly encouragements to scrutinize, examine, and probe the meaning of scripture.

What impresses me most is that Jesus and the God about whom he teaches doesn't seem the least bit afraid of being exposed by our scrutiny. Exposure is a means for comprehension and cognition, never a means for jeopardizing God.

I remember just a few decades ago, as humans first began their quest of the unknown universe in space there was much trepidation among many people of faith. For the insecure, the potential that astronauts might explore the outer reaches of the heavens was threatening. What would happen, they feared, when the astronauts passed by the "heavens" where God resided and found no one at home? Haven't we been there and done that before? For God to encourage an openness and exploration of the created universe demonstrates a God who is secure in being God.

It's not about Jesus; it's what Jesus is about.

For decades, bible study has been my foray. I have pursued it with a passion bordering on obsession. I have attended bible studies. I have designed bible studies. I have taught bible studies. I have sometimes avoided bible studies when I felt they presented the bible without introspection or compassion or with too much entrenchment. In my capacity as teaching minister in a number of congregations, bible study and Christian education remain as a focus for my ministry.

In an attempt to establish appropriate and adequate teaching resources and methods to be helpful to both adults and teens, my search is never ending. I look for certain curriculums or materials that will meet particular criteria that I feel are both necessary and helpful in leading people along their faith journeys. Those that I have found adequate have the following commonalities:

- They encourage students to inquire about faith issues.
- They raise appropriate questions rather than give pat answers
- They examine faith in the context of real life situations.
- They ask, "What difference does it make?"
- They consider what Jesus is about, not just about Jesus
- They are relevant as well as reverent.

In my classes, I had many students who were quite knowledgeable about Jesus. They knew who he was, where he lived, what he said. This they learned in Church school. When they stumbled, it was because they could not come to grips with the relevancy of his message for their lives. "What difference did it make?" Share any scriptural text with them and they were very comfortable talking about the text, its historical background, the people in the text, and the meaning of the text in the "context" of the text.

Even teenagers could handle this aspect of study. But when we got around to asking what difference that text made to them and how it affected the living of their lives, they often grew silent. It was as if asked to talk about Martians. I felt I was treading in forbidden territory. What right did I have to ask such questions? Wasn't it enough to know about Jesus without the intrusion of knowing what Jesus was about?

I wasn't content. How could blind acceptance ever be a condition upon which faith could grow? I eventually discovered that I was working with students under the pretense of at least two false assumptions:

• **Assumption one** – To say you are Christian is to be a Christian. That's all that is necessary. I assumed that my students, some with little more than church school education, had a well formed Christian faith. They had all the marks of being Christian – baptized, brought up in Christian homes, attended church regularly, held Christian "attitudes and ethics", all the expected and normal criteria one would assume as marking a Christian. I was wrong. Despite meeting the criteria, they were not yet Christian, nor was I. These students knew about Jesus, they knew about his life and ministry and could easily convince themselves and me that because they "believed in Jesus" that was the sole criteria for becoming Christian. It's a start, but not conclusive. Just because we know about Jesus doesn't translate into knowing what Jesus is about. The mark of being a Christian is to show evidence that one not only knows about Jesus, but also is actively and continually engaged in "doing" what Jesus is about. This is a core philosophy in teaching teenagers; raising the questions about relevance and challenging them in dialogue about the difference faith might make in their lives.

• **Assumption two** – I assumed that my students wanted to know more about becoming Christian. In fact, they didn't. They seemed satisfied by their status quo. To learn more about what the bible says was legitimate fodder for bible study. But to be challenged to act or respond to what the bible says, to seek change based on scripture teachings, to question what difference the scriptures might make in their life decisions and actions, well, that was going too far. It was not necessary. In brief, I assumed they wanted to be challenged, but they wanted to be comforted.

The premise of this chapter is that no one specific set of assumptions are sufficient for teenagers. Knowing about Jesus is not the same as knowing what Jesus is about. Knowledge is not wisdom without practical considerations. Christian faith is as much about how God intends us to live in the world as it is about knowing who God is. What would be the point of ignoring the applications of faith in our real world, if that, indeed, is the world into which God has put us?

This brief introduction is meant to encourage you, the teacher of faith formation for teenagers, to challenge your students at every point in their confirmation education. Raise questions with them. Challenge them to defend their faith. Get them to consider alternatives to faith. Debate with them the options they choose. Make them articulate what they believe. Only with dialogue will these teens acquire what Kenda Dean refers to as *"consequential faith."*

7

BELONGING - THE NEED FOR ACCEPTANCE

The Key to Faith Formation is Knowing Where You Belong

Building a community is like gardening.
You plant the seeds, and pray something
worthwhile will happen. Fertilizer helps. Care is
indispensable. But you can't force things
to grow.

---anonymous

(Some of the material in this chapter appeared in an earlier publication of mine, entitled Youth at Risk.-Pilgrim Press, 2003)

Some years ago, there was a popular television series entitled Cheers. Each episode of the show opened with the song, "*Where Everybody Knows Your Name.*" Cheers was a Boston bar, frequented by a variety of zany characters, but one where everybody, despite whatever flaws or eccentricities they may have, was equally welcomed and accepted. Everyone belonged. Its popularity, I suspect, was precisely because the audience could identify with the feeling of belonging, a place where *everybody knows your name.*

Belonging is a crucial element in the forming of human community. Feeling included into a community of one sort or another has been a necessity and a condition that humans have never been able to deny themselves. We often try to exert our independence; we tell others we don't need anyone, we are sufficient unto ourselves. We only fool ourselves. The focus of much counseling by therapists, including clergy, is to enable people to feel there is a place where they belong and accepted for who they are unconditionally.

Clergy, especially, recognize the connection between forming human relationships and the ability to form a relationship with God. The idea of belonging is more than acknowledging a place to be; it's an attitude, a posture, a sensitivity. Only after feeling that *somebody knows your name* can an individual hope to survive in an alien world. It is the same posture one adopts with faith; knowing that God knows your name; feeling that God cares enough to know your name and accept you, is the foundation of a faith based relationship with God

"…what is man that thou art
mindful of him,
and the son of man that thou dost care for him?"

(Psalm 8:4 RSV)

Right from the get-go, God recognizes that "man" needs company. *"Then the Lord God said. 'it is not good that man should be alone"* (Genesis 2:18 RSV). Living a life in isolation can be devastating even for the strongest and most mature among us. Imagine its effects upon those just beginning to emerge into maturity, the most vulnerable among us; the adolescent. The striving to belong and be accepted into a community is so intense among adolescents that when it is not present or acknowledged in positive, sustaining ways, it often breaks out in damaging ways. Behavior becomes self-destructive. Anger is unleashed. Aggressive conduct becomes uncontrollable. Promiscuity runs rampant. Consequences may be only temporary, but sometimes even brief encounters have lasting effects. For the impressionable and easily influenced adolescent, when the healthy community of acceptance is not accessible, alternatives become an attraction – gangs, cults, drugs, rebellion, deviant behaviors.

Teens that have a sense of belonging to a particular group learn a variety of lessons from this association. Teen groups can offer both positive and negative influences. Teens learn to evaluate themselves based upon perception of their peers in these groups. The members of the peer group serve essentially as a mirror, providing feedback about behavior and personalities to individual group members. Teens who are part of a group with positive goals can gain confidence in social settings by learning the value of cooperation and accountability within the group.

Teenagers who belong to a positive group usually are better prepared to resist negative peer pressure from marginalized outside sources. Teens in positive groups develop a strong sense of self empowered by others. Teens who participate in negative groups respond in a similar manner, but reflect an adverse attitude about themselves and others. Mentors who get to know teenage peer groups, and recognize their characteristics both positive and negative, are better able to identify how peers influence each other. It is always helpful to know to which groups teens associate.

Teenagers who do not feel a sense of belonging from family and friends will pursue intimacy in unhealthy ways. Teens crave affection and a sense of acceptance and will begin to experiment with these feelings. Because teens are unfamiliar with and have no practice in intimate relationships, they usually end up disappointed. Mentors need to acknowledge these feelings and encourage teens to talk about them.

Create Christian community.

Creating a healthy community in which the adolescent feels he/she belongs is an essential first step for the confirmation educator. The Christian community aspires toward being a community of inclusion, which is precisely the model God sets before us. If kids learn what they live, which all good research seems to indicate, and if they are going to learn that a loving God accepts them and can be trusted with their faith, they must first experience acceptance and trust as part of a community to which they feel they belong. Herein lays the direct connection between the spiritual nurture and the developmental needs of the adolescent. We will not be successful at nurturing the faith formation of adolescents without recognizing and acknowledging their developmental need to belong. A key to healthy development lies in the creation of a community of belonging for only in the context of that kind of community will adolescents be open and accepting of Christian relationships. Our hope of creating a trusting relationship in a God that is yet to be recognized lies in our ability to provide a trusting community that is already recognized.

Despite which model of confirmation education the congregation chooses – traditional or experiential – establishing an accepting community and an atmosphere of belonging is a priority. People assume, with few exceptions, that those entering into confirmation education be baptized. Baptism, as an act of inclusion, probably has little meaning for them since, as infants, they did not choose it, it was chosen for them. They have yet to discover its meaning. Baptism, by its very nature, seeks to embrace the person into a community. The congregation declares the child is included in the community of Christians.

But the congregation must initiate and then demonstrate that inclusion. It isn't automatic just because the preacher declared it as part of the sacrament. The confirmation program is an ideal place to exercise that option; a time when the adolescent can grow in awareness of what it feels like to belong and to learn to trust the tenets of Christian faith in a context of belonging to a community. These two characteristics – belonging and trusting - happen at the same time or they don't happen at all. Inclusion is a prerequisite of Christian practice. Faith formation with teenagers happens best in the context of an accepting community that actively practices Christian customs.

Create an intentional community.

Creating the sense of belonging must be intentional. The group takes the initiative. The teen merely responds to the invitation of the group. The following characteristics contribute toward creating that community. The list is suggestive, but surely not exhaustive, of very specific attitudes, behaviors, and attributes that the confirmation leader exhibits that contribute toward creating an atmosphere in which acceptance thrives and belonging is cultivated.

1. Awareness of adolescent fears.

Adolescents are plagued with fears of all sorts and kinds; some real and some imaginary or concocted. The fear of rejection, fear of embarrassment, fear of being different, fear of failure, fear of being "found out", all dominate their relationships and personal worth. The accepting community intentionally reaches out to the teenager with an attitude of acceptance and belonging "just as you are."

2. Allow for mistakes.

Mistakes happen often and with great frequency for adolescents. Admitting their mistakes is not easy. You help the confirmand by your willingness to tolerate mistakes. Toleration means accepting without condemning but not condoning the mistake.

If you, as the confirmation educator, are particularly bothered by people who are constantly making mistakes, drawing wrong conclusions, and over estimating abilities, then you are the wrong person to be leading a bunch of adolescents. Teenagers mess up a lot. They make mistakes, and plenty of them. Among their greatest attributes is the propensity to do the wrong thing at the wrong time. Any teens, worth their salt and acting normally, are going to pick the wrong solution to some of life's easiest problems. They can't help it.

Despite that they have little life experience, adolescents often act overconfident. My granddaughter, fast approaching adolescence, is a good example. No matter the activity or subject, if I suggest a way of doing it, her response inevitably is, "Yeah, I know that." It takes considerable humility on her part to ask for help, even after she gets the wrong answer or can't figure out how something works. Admitting mistakes or showing ignorance is never an easy task, it suggests helplessness. Often young teens refuse to acknowledge mistakes and continue to plunge ahead despite screwing up.

The astute confirmation educator, in creating an accepting atmosphere, does not condone mistakes, but recognizes they will exist and does not take umbrage when they happen. A willingness to accept mistakes sets the stage for building trust and a sense of belonging which is so essential for establishing a foundation for faith formation.

3. Accept failure.

Failure cannot be a reason for exclusion from the community. An accepting community sends the message that if teens are encouraged to try new things, harbor new thoughts, take on new responsibilities, stretch their potential; you assure them that failure will not exclude them; that they can make these mistakes without recrimination or rejection. The confirmation group offers a place where adolescents are rescued from consequences of bad decisions and encouraged to try again. Give them second chances.

Young people often exaggerate the pitfalls of failure. They have inflated expectations of their abilities. When they are reminded of blemishes in their talents or skills, they take it personally. They have difficulty distinguishing between the act and the person who criticizes.

My daughter tried out for the Junior High cheerleading squad. She practiced and practiced, but when it came time for the auditions, she failed miserably. She couldn't jump high enough. She dropped her pompom. Her cartwheel resembled a potato chip. She was devastated. She wouldn't come out of her room for the whole week-end. Sure she was embarrassed, but even more so, she couldn't handle disappointment. She was not only a cheer leading failure, she was a human failure. She personalized the event. She even blamed the judges for being unqualified. She got over it. Everything passes with time.

It is not easy for mature adults to understand the universalizing characteristics that overwhelm adolescents. If I told my daughter that she was good on the clarinet, and was the best soccer goalie in Junior High, it wouldn't alleviate that failing at cheerleading meant failure in life, period. You want the adolescent to get past the feeling, to get over it, but they just may not be ready so soon because of the intensity of the feeling.

Then there are those times you are sure the young person is using failure as a means to test your acceptance. When she feigns failure over something insignificant, like doing poorly on a test in school, or forgetting to clean up her room after you asked three times repeatedly, or not getting an invitation to the Valentines party, you might conclude that she is merely testing your willingness to remain accepting of her despite her failures. If the test doesn't go well; she might conclude that she is, in fact, unacceptable. The feelings of failure remain intense despite that she is using them as a test.

In the context of the confirmation experience, when there is a bonding occurring between student and congregation, this testing becomes particularly significant. Missing classes, not attending church, and shying away from time spent with mentors may be intentional as a means for exploring just how accepting and forgiving the congregation will be. The congregation responds, not by condoning or excusing the failures, but rather with a sense that belonging to the community is unconditional. The confirmand may have failed in responsibility, but is not a failure as a person.

4. Defeat criticism.

Teens are extremely sensitive to criticism (an understatement, to be sure). They have their own interpretation of events and a strong sense of their own worth. It's a fragile relationship easily upset by criticism. Teens view criticism and the person criticizing as one and the same. It is always thought to be unfair ("the coach doesn't like me"). Criticism isolates the adolescent and isolation is the antithesis of belonging.

Being naturally self-centered, adolescents are particularly sensitive to criticism. Suggest to my granddaughter that she was rude to her friend and acted rather selfish, and she will burst into tears and run from the room. Criticism catches the young person at a very vulnerable time. They already have intense feelings of insecurity. They may pretend they don't care what others say or think, but that is only a subterfuge. Actually they care very much, sometimes so much so that they will not let it show, bury the hurt feelings, and act them out later in negative ways. Adult criticism may be intended as a means to encourage growth, to change behavior for the better, or alter attitudes from negative to positive, but in reality it is perceived as a threat by the sensitive teen

Teenagers view the person criticizing as unfair. (the teacher plays favorites).Defensiveness is the adolescents' reaction to criticism and defensiveness cuts off all avenues for constructive conversation. As a leader of confirmation, it is best that you learn to bite your tongue. The temptation to correct errant ways often backfires. Constantly pointing out wrongdoing leads easily to a habit of criticism. Criticism instills shame in a person and shame translates into feelings of stupidity and worthlessness. As well, outlaw name calling, put downs, and scape-goating from the members of the class. Your goal is the creation of a community of acceptance where members feel they belong. Only in that context are the students able to understand that Christian faith is inclusive and accepting.

5. Defeat alienation

Blaming others and scape-goating are common ploys of adolescents. When not living up to expectations, their own or others, teens are quick to blame, provide alibis, or fault conditions beyond their control ("All the other kids are bigger than me. How can I compete fairly when the coach plays favorites?"). Resist the immediate desire to chastise. Instead provide encouragement to find options or alternatives to what they present as obstacles. Help them meet their own responsibilities without rejection.

6. Be non-judgmental.

It is not your responsibility as confirmation leader to become best friends with each of your students. As a matter of fact, it is discouraged. Don't even try to act like one of them. You are the adult and ultimately that is what they expect from you; to act like an adult.

Adults can be very judgmental of adolescents. It's hard not to be. But refrain as much as possible and instead merely attempt to know each one as a person. Avoid getting into relationships with predetermined attitudes and opinions.

We are usually quick to form opinions about how young people ought to act. Our prejudices flow easily, especially about their choice of clothing and accessories, their music, their friends, and their lack of motivation. We want to fix things; impose our set of values on them, and make them clones of ourselves. These attitudes may remain unsaid, but they have a sneaky way of revealing themselves through your spontaneous reactions. Even unsaid, they are judgmental nonetheless.

You are an advocate for the adolescent. As confirmation leader, your task is to encourage growth in students, to enable them to become the best they can, to make changes they need to make or want to make, to develop in ways specific for their growth, not yours. Learn to think differently. Think as a facilitator and become student centered, not teacher centered. Knowing what they think and responding non-judgmentally is essential for instilling new thoughts in your students. As they express opinions about faith and life, allow for dialogue. Dialogue encourages the student to hear what they are saying as well as what others are saying which becomes a channel for arriving at new thoughts. Dialogue is the principle means for achieving a consequential faith.

7. learn to listen

Learning to be a good listener may be the pinnacle attribute of the confirmation teacher. The art of listening presupposes that you take an intense interest in the adolescent and the act of listening is probably the best indication you can give the teen of that concern. Kids love it when people listen to them. It makes them feel good about themselves and, in turn, creates in them a positive attitude toward you for enabling that feel-good attitude. It takes stamina to listen to teenagers instead of talking at them, but it goes a long way toward establishing that sense of belonging and acceptance unconditionally.

Your willingness to listen to them is a new experience; they are not used to that kind of relationship with adults. Mostly they are talked at, not listened to. Listening is an act of respect. Gaining that respect enables you, the teacher, to be more influential in their lives and be seen more as a trusting person. What you share about the Christian faith becomes more credible to the teen when done in a trusting relationship.

8. Be non – competitive.

In the real world, the one teens face each day, much time and great effort must be expended competing against each other - better grades, winning teams, better looking, more cool, more popular, etc. The confirmation group ought to be one experience in which cooperation instead of competition is the driving force. Belonging depends upon being accepted for who one is at present, not for who one might become later. Building and accepting community requires using non-competitive games and simulations that encourage teens to work together toward a common goal. Avoid competition, unless absolutely necessary.

All of the above are skills the confirmation teacher will employ to build a confidence level in those participating in the confirmation class program. When they sense that they are accepted and belong to a group, teens become more trusting. They willingly accept that faith formation is not an intrusion in their lives, but rather a support, a means for becoming a more complete person, an experience of unconditional care, all of which meets the expectations of both the confirmand and the Christian community into which they are invited to join.

Fear of abandonment.

For the adolescent, the fear of being lost can be overwhelming. Social psychologists tell us that the greatest fear of childhood, even into the teen years, is abandonment. Born into a world where they are totally dependent upon others for every need, young people rely on the security that they will be taken care of; that parents or other adults can be counted on, and they will not be left alone. Teenagers may not own up to this feeling, but it's there. Real or imagined, the feeling of abandonment cuts to the very heart and soul of every living creature, so much so that when left alone, a child's will to survive might be altered beyond repair.

These qualities suggest conditions under which teenagers will thrive. Clearly they will respond well to the confirmation program by being part of a community that understands who they are and acts accordingly. Unless the community emulates these qualities, the adolescent may choose not to join or drop out of after exposure. Belonging is not a prerequisite for becoming a Christian, but rest assured that in the context of confirmation belonging is a feeling that must be present when forming Christian relationships.

Our God is a God of lost causes. God seems to thrive and show the most compassion when resolving blunders, undoing our mistakes, or fixing the messed-up situations into which we get ourselves. This is the God that permeates the life of our Christian community and it is the God of which we want every teen in our care to get to know.

The Christian community aspires toward being a community of inclusion. That is precisely the model God sets before us. We learn to include others because God included us. We invite others into the community because we know firsthand the value of belonging. It is the very concept from which faith is born and nurtured in our teenagers.

Tips for building healthy relationships with teens
(summery sheet of information)

1. Show respect. Learn their names. Recognize each adolescent as an individual and don't play favorites.
2. Be patient. Building trust and rapport takes time. Take your clues from their timelines.
3. Establish clear boundaries. No need for you to be a best friend. Stay in your role as adult. Don't discuss your personal life.
4. Be consistent. Adolescents do best with regular structure. They are not good at too much "free time". Be

consistent when implementing limits and tolerable behavior.

5. Listen. Pay attention and hear what they are saying even if you don't agree. Avoid giving too much advice.
6. Recognize they are growing up in a different era than you. Enough said.
7. Don't embarrass. Embarrassment is the worst debasement. Pull them aside for personal conversation when necessary.
8. Don't tell adolescents how they should feel. Invalidating their feelings and perspectives makes it unlikely they will share with you again.
9. Avoid blame. Even when the adolescent shares some responsibility for a problem, be careful about laying blame too quickly.
10. Invite teens to suggest topics or activities that are relevant to whatever the subject might be. Teens will learn what they want to learn. When the teen feels an investment in the subject, they are more likely to learn about it.
11. Where ever possible, give teens a chance to produce something that matters. Having to complete a task purely for the sake of completion quickly becomes boring for the student.
12. Give teenagers a chance to explain what is going on before launching into a tirade of judgment and discipline. Listening to their side creates trust and respect.

How to Enjoy Confirmation (for students)

Just as the adult may be anxious about sharing a relationship with an adolescent and want to back out of it, so also does the confirmand share some anxiety that might contribute to saying no to the whole experience. Confirmation isn't a chore. Take advantage of the experience and it can be pleasant. As a student in confirmation you can actually learn to like it, but that may take adherence to some basic principles.

- *Loose the attitude*: you don't have to be in confirmation class. It's a choice. It's not punishment. It's a new experience. Loosen up. Being rude or disrespectful will make a good experience feel horrible.
- *Show appreciation to the teacher*: No body is paid to be part of confirmation, certainly not the teacher or volunteer adults. They do it because they like young people. You can "like" them back.
- *Make new friends*: You will probably know some kids in the class, but there will also be ones you need to get to know. It's a good way to make new friends.

8

FAITH FORMATION

"Faith is to believe what you do not see;
the reward of this faith is to see what you believe."

--St Augustine

"Hear. O Israel, the Lord our God is one Lord;
and you shall love the Lord your
God with all your heart, and with all your soul,
and with all your might.

(Deuteronomy 6: 4-5 RSV)

So what is faith?

I once asked my granddaughter this very question. Quick as a flash she responded, *"Believing something you can't prove."* My granddaughter isn't the only one who thinks like this. I have known many rational, mature, and educated adults who, when pressed to talk about faith, feel the same as my granddaughter. It's like the grownup who still believes in Santa Clause just because he likes it, not because he has thought much about it. It's believing something your rational mind can't prove; something so farfetched that it's beyond reason, but somehow has become a part of your psyche. As one person described it, *"faith is counting on something far down in your heart that gets you to accept something that you know your intellect concludes is false."* Many people with an accredited rational education believe that to rely on faith you have to close your mind, put your intellect to sleep, and ignore the conclusions of science and research. And so they do.

Faith without explanation.

"Faith is believing what you want to believe, yet cannot prove." I have met many enlightened Christian folk for whom this understanding is paramount to their religious practice. Don't over-think the idea, they claim, it is sufficient to believe whatever you want, no explanation is required. It's just a matter of faith. Embracing faith means to stop thinking. No explanation is adequate and none is required or expected. When you try to explain it, it loses its value as faith.

This misinterpretation of the concept of faith runs rampant. It serves to confuse rather than enlighten. Eventually the mature Christian has to move beyond fanciful thinking and toward mature faith. Come out of the dark and into the light. It does not contradict reason. It is not dreaming. It does not make all things believable nor meaning dysfunctional. In fact, faith is not contrary to the human intellect but rather complements it. People exercise faith every day, often without realizing it.

Perhaps the confusion stems from the wrong definition of faith. By starting with a false definition, they ask the wrong questions, deal with the wrong problems, and end up with the wrong answers. The expression *"just have faith, it will work out"* is used often to encourage people facing serious problems. It's like saying there is nothing you can do, but it will turn out all right despite you. It is an attempt to alleviate concerns without substance. When faith is without foundation, however, it discourages more than encourages; people become disillusioned and suspicious.

Perhaps the best word we can use to translate the Greek word for faith "pistis" into contemporary English is *"trust."* The substance of faith is trust. Faith by itself has no real meaning. Faith can only be understood in a context. It is used to describe a condition of trustworthiness in a person, object or experience. A couple of classic illustrations help us understand the difference between faith founded in trust and blind belief or wishful thinking

Find the chair closest to you. Look at it carefully. Examine its design. Is it sound? Is it well constructed? Are the materials used of highest quality? Will the glue hold together? Will it support your weight?

Most likely you have chosen a chair that will support you. That's blind belief. You applied logic to make an informed intellectual decision but you still don't know if the chair is trustworthy.

Now sit in the chair. That's faith. Intellectual assent only goes so far, Faith requires we put our beliefs into action.

We also need to recognize that real faith depends upon its object. You are walking through the woods when you come upon a small stream. A single plank spans the steam. You must decide if you will walk across the plank. The moment you step on the plank, you are exercising faith. But whether you get across safely depends on the plank. You may have considerable faith, but if the plank is rotten, you land in the water. Real faith depends on the object. There is trust in the object, in this case, the plank. If the plank holds up, it becomes the object of your faith.

Faith is a human endeavor. It is not the sole property of religion to the exclusion of all other human activity. It has practical considerations that people make use of every day. Although faith is beyond our ability to extract it in any physical form, we can experience how it works.

So what is faith? Because we can't explicitly define and observe faith as in a scientific experiment, we can observe when it is operable in human life. Faith is like your eyesight. There must be something there for you to see, an object upon which your eyes focus. The way you know you have eyesight is that you see something. Faith, then is an assurance that the object is real, you can count on it being what you think it is and your actions relative to the object are trustworthy.

Faith has always been integral, if not central, to religion. Religious beliefs depend on faith. Religious faith, like your eyesight, depends on the object upon which you focus your faith. The object of faith is God. Religious faith is depended upon the credibility of the object of your faith. For the Christian, this is God; we have faith or trust in God. We don't just believe that God is real, we know God as real. When we know that God is trustworthy because of previous experience with God, then we experience faith. Faith is trusting in God. But it is not a blind trust. Faith is knowing that God is real and that you can trust in the promises of God.

The book of Hebrews talks about faith as the "*substance*" of things hoped for and as the "*evidence*" of things not seen. Both words carry with them a sense of reality. Faith does not make God real; faith is our response to the reality of God. It is not the amount of faith that is important but the worthiness of the object – can God be trusted?

What can you expect from teenagers?

Faith is not the exclusive domain of adults; it is pervasive for all people including teenagers. Our task, thus far, has focused on methods by which we can nurture faith in God among our teenaged population. But the problem becomes one of knowing to what degree this is possible.

Some thinkers relate the work of spiritual nurture of teenagers to the metaphor of a potter. The potter forms a lump of clay into a pot or mug. In the same way teachers and parents often think of adolescents in their "formative" years as recipients of learning, ready to be shaped into whatever mold the adult or society or the church chooses for them. Formation brings to mind shaping or molding, influencing the faith potential of teenagers into something that resembles an ideal.

When my own daughters were in girl scouts, I observed an excellent program of developmental education. It involves learning that takes into account the ability of the learner at that moment while at the same time moving the learner onward. They start with simple tasks; learning to cook Jell-O, sewing a button, climbing a hill. Then through a system of teaching, learning, and rewards, scouts gain more sophisticated knowledge about their expertise. From boiling water and making pudding, they learn nutrition and how to cook a balanced meal. From helping each other cross a stream in the woods, they learn to impact society by renovating a homeless shelter. It is not a perfect system, but it does help the scout grow towards maturity, and it does it slowly over time and in stages.

It can be the same with faith formation. It doesn't happen haphazardly or all at once. It does not come solely from the confirmation experience or by being a member of the youth group that meets once each month. It happens through intentional design, steadfast innovation, and attention to content that is reinforced week after week, year after year.

The challenge of consequential faith.

Mark and I met for lunch. Mark is the youth pastor of a local congregation.

Right after ordering our food, Mark remained unusually quiet. I noticed what I thought was a pensive look on his face.

"What's up Mark, "I asked?

"I don't know if all this makes a difference," he remarked.

I was intrigued. "Tell me more," I encouraged him.

"Does it really matter? I use creative bible study. I engage the kids in mission. They participate in the worship services. They come regularly to youth group. But I don't think these kids are getting anything; certainly not any spiritual nurture."

I gave this conversation much consideration. I understood Mark's frustration. Both he and I and many others desperately want teenagers to experience faith the way he and I did. But teens are not mature adults. A consequential mature faith remains an expectation for their future and a difficult challenge for any teacher to undertake, but just because a Christian faith is difficult for teenagers to grasp, doesn't mean that we give up trying.

Trust is the foundation for faith. If this is true, which I believe it is, it is also true that how we learn to practice trust is the launching point for enabling teens to engage if faith. Trust is not unique to the spiritual province. Our task as religious educators is to acknowledge that trust is basic to human need and is practiced to one degree or another in all areas of teen's lives. We begin to shape religious faith with teenagers when we can capitalize on those experiences of trusting already available to teenagers. To the degree that adolescents' begin to form trusting relationships between themselves and others, to the same degree they can begin to transform that trusting relationship to God.

Practicing faith.

Educational experts agree, experience is the best teacher. Doing something by oneself is the foundation of learning. Personal experience reinforces learning. You are what you do. It has been demonstrated repeatedly that we retain very little of what we hear, perhaps a bit more of what we read, but almost all of what we experience. Physicians, for example, are well aware of this principle. Despite how many years of study and a whole host of degrees, it is the experience of practicing medicine that greatly improves their diagnosis and treatment ability.

Throughout our life, from cradle to the grave, our lives revolve around practices. We fill our daily lives with habits, drills, exercises, and customs that we employ as we face each situation. We practice playing the piano and we get better. We practice forming relationships and we get better. We practice ice skating and we get better. From cooking to quantum physics, football to fencing, ballet to brick laying, all skills require practice to master. We each have our own set of natural abilities which make us more suited to certain activities. Without practice, however, we quickly become dormant with only the potential of becoming great. Without practice we wouldn't be able to carry out our daily activities like cooking for our families, riding a bike, or working to earn a living. All require a level of practice to perform properly. It may be an overstatement that practice makes us perfect. Perfection is not always our goal, but good practice always makes us better.

Where faith begins.

Teaching teenagers about religious faith begins by acknowledging that faith is inherent in their daily lives.

They have grown up learning to trust; trusting their parents, trusting teachers, trusting friends, trusting in any and all sorts of people, experiences, and objects. Trust is not a new experience for teenagers. It is part and parcel of everything they experience. Once they learn the art of trusting, they are ready for faith; a faith that trusts God. Thus begins their practice of faith.

Despite that teens rely heavily on trusting relationships, the potential for spirituality remains a giant leap. The transition from faith in family to faith in God is like crossing a chasm as wide as the Grand Canyon. The confirmation educator remains open to any flicker of interest; any hint there might be hope. If parents and teachers can establish credibility with this skeptical audience in nonreligious areas, there's a chance we might see that squinted face that discovers something never given consideration before – a glimmer of religious appreciation. "Hey, wait a minute. I may be missing something. You listen to ... God?"

We have a duty to our students' minds, but we have a more profound duty to their souls. We can sensitize them. Our task as apostles to the young is to lead them, like God, to understand and express the self-not merely the "sometime spirit" that emerges by chance during a dutiful hour in worship, but the spirit that *is* the child's true self. But that will require a major conversion, in teachers and administrators, from our pervasively pragmatic and efficient mind-set. It requires practice.

Centering on the spiritual. Practicing the faith in steps.

At the elementary age, rather than instruct children about heavy theological concepts like sin or redemption or the trinity, let us teach them, once a week at least, ways of relaxing and centering themselves; opening themselves to God. Very young children are fairly good candidates for meditation, and receptive prayer. They are less uptight, less defensive, and more imaginative. According to Jesus, they are always in the Kingdom. Teach them to feel it, enjoy it, revel in it, and perhaps even remain in it. Practice the art of faith.

It is well documented that children learn far faster when their curiosity is piqued, when they are given not answers but problems and sent off in quest of their own answers. It is not as efficient as teach and repeat back, but the God we are trying to sensitize them to is not as efficient as we'd like, either.

Let children's liturgies be fun. For God's sake, don't preach to them. Let each one tell what God looks like; let each one tell what they like about Jesus. Don't do it for them. By the time for confirmation, they should be ready for a weekend retreat--perhaps not yet a purely supernatural one, but one where they can break down their ego-defenses in safety, reach out, be vulnerable and unafraid for a while.

In high school, we ought to give at least some time to the same kinds of activities. One such exercise is "trust," where one student falls backward and another catches him or her. Activities that challenge teens to "talk" about trust issues will expose their readiness to transition trust to religious practice.

The concept of "practice" is the foundation of faith formation. Faith formation is a life-long pursuit. We are always "becoming "Christians. We never fully arrive. If we think that any one program, much less the one or two years teenagers spend in confirmation, is sufficient to fully nurture a mature and viable Christian faith, we are misinformed. Faith formation is a life venture at every age and stage of human development. We are forever practicing our faith. Consider confirmation as one step along the road.

Becoming a Christian, regardless at what stage a person begins, takes diligence and practice, Faith formation is best served by practice. There are "things" that we do that serve to enhance our faith. There more we do them, the more we grow. These things include but are not limited to the practice of faith in worship, celebration of holy days, participating in prayer, bible reading, and serving those in need beyond our immediate congregations. Each activity serves to nurture faith formation. They provides the practice we need to become proficient.

There is no discrepancy between knowing and doing the Christian faith. It is interesting to note that the bible makes reference to faith formation in a number of ways, almost always from the perspective of faith *formation* rather than faith *information*. Christian faith does not stand in opposition to knowing or believing. But a person may have considerable knowledge about God, about Jesus, about the mission and ministry of the church, or even be literate in Christian theology but still not have an active, ongoing relationship with God. Faith formation lays emphasis on the awe and wonder of God with experiences that connect the person to something transcendent and of ultimate concern.

Klaus Issler in his work *Wasting Time with God,* (Intervarsity Press, 2001) describes faith formation as *"focusing on the ongoing, dynamic, and transforming aspects of a walk with God."* With the experience of practicing the faith – worship, study, missions, prayer, and writing – we enrich faith formation. Rehearsing the "business" of faith helps to ingrain faith forcefully while at the same time teaching the tenets of the faith. Just knowing the contents of the bible does not make a committed Christian. As one writer stated; it's not *about* Jesus, it's what Jesus is *about*. The challenge for the religious educator of teenagers is to encourage the teen to have both a walk and a talk with God. This transition is never an easy endeavor.

Knowing the practice profile of a congregation – what practices are flourishing, what practices seem anemic and need revitalization – is a beginning strategy for teenagers. Before inviting teens into a Christian way of life, we need to have some sense of what this life entails and how it shapes the lives of people of faith. Know what practices are important to the congregation.

Faith formation, not evangelism.

Spiritual formation and evangelism are opposites. They are not even closely related. Evangelism is proselytizing. Its foundation lies in spreading the gospel through personal witness. It seeks to convert non-believers into believers. It is exclusive; it promotes a single belief to the exclusion of all other beliefs or opinions. Evangelism tactics are employed, for instance, to convince non-Christians to become Christians. Evangelism provides no options, makes no room for divergent considerations, and opts for a single truth with the elimination of all others. Evangelism, as I understand it, is entrenched in a single perspective - only Christianity matters to the exclusion of all other faiths. That's okay.

Faith formation, on the other hand, has as its purpose to encourage growth in faith rather than insist on conversion or change. It begins with the assumption that the person (or adolescent) has already been introduced to Christen faith and has an inkling; an emerging sense of the basics of that faith. Faith formation is not a beginning point, but rather an ongoing process of growth.

When the scriptures speak about an "increase" in love or the increase in knowledge or the increase in faith, the assumption is that the spiritual experience of the person is already formed, but needs nurture to grow, to increase. Faith from the "formative" perspective is never fulfilled; it is always in the process of becoming, growing deeper, becoming more mature.

A walk with God.

When television first became popular in the 50's, the commercials were thirty-second live logical arguments for buying a particular product. The marketers' counted of "facts" to convince people to purchase their products. Those commercials were not that effective. Soon thereafter the marketers learned that human stories of people using the product in the context of their lives was a much stronger message, one to which people could identify and consequently connect with the product being offered.

Religious educators learned from this experience. Just as advertisements use stories to connect with people's lives, so also does the bible present stories for the same purpose -to connect with people's lives. The scriptures are stories of people interacting with God. They are powerful, persuasive stories able to impact and even change lives. The content of the biblical stories comes alive as people intersect the story of God with the story of their own lives. A "walk" with God is an exercise in finding connection between what God is about and what the person is about. Faith formation intentionally shapes us inside the story of God. It is to find trustworthiness in God and to respond to that trust with faithfulness. This is the activity with which we want to engage our teenagers; to encourage an intersection to happen between their lives and the experience of God.

The activity of faith formation.

Faith formation is not a program, but rather a 24/7 life walk. God is forming us all the time and the activity of faith formation is always happening. Our efforts to understand this activity has a dual dimension: (1) We try to understand what the Lord is always doing and (2) we want to replicate this dimension in our specific programing with teenagers. The following is an effort to combine these principles in a working model.

1. Faith formation is goal oriented: Paul describes the goal orientation this way. "...and to know the love of Christ which surpasses knowledge that you may be filled with all the fullness of God." (Ephesians 3:19 RSV). But because we do not experience "arriving at the goal," it is difficult to image what that might look like. This goal orientation has one implication for all people involved in faith formation; we are to be incredibly patient and hopeful. A faith journey for the adolescent is always a jagged path of ups and downs. But just as God patiently walks with us toward maturity, we patiently and hopefully walk with our young people, keeping our eyes fixed on the goal.
2. Faith formation requires a relationship: Too often Christian education programs (i.e. Confirmation) tells teens a great deal about God without enabling teens to form a relationship with God. Faith formation needs to reshape hearts to receive God's love more fully. When we place too much emphasis upon knowledge

about God, it is at the expense of too little emphasis on formatting a relationship with God. When there is a tendency to increase knowledge it often serves to stifle relationships. Teen faith formation depends upon trust and relationships beginning between peers and mentors and transitioning to God.

3. Faith Formation requires spiritual discipline: The Christian faith calls people to live in a way that is consistent with our concept of what God requires. These spiritual disciplines are activities that declare "I want to be more like Christ," Those who actively propose the concepts of Christian practices (from the work of Craig Dykstra and Dorothy C. Bass) emphasize that teens need to be directly engaged in these practices - worship, prayer, generosity, hospitality, scripture reading and dialogue, promoting justice, thanksgiving, gift giving. All these are a part of a larger fabric of spiritual disciplines that combine to carry out the Lord's formative work.
4. Create a village for faith formation: The faith formation of teenagers is enhanced specifically through intergenerational and family based learning. It is not acceptable for adults and children to go separate ways – children to Sunday school, teenagers to youth groups, and adults to worship. We need the entire community's attention upon faith to shape teenagers in faith formation. The church must be a "faith village" where parents, grandparents and all others assume responsibility for the nurture of faith of their teen population. Encounter with the living God is hearing, seeing, tasting, and touching God's presence in one another, in mutual pronouncing and listening by all ages together. This exposure helps to immunize teens against literal interpretations of the scriptures.

The above processes of nurturing faith for teens suggest very specific strategies. There are many resources and curriculums that outline such strategies. Most particularly they are the work done by three studies on youth ministry and adolescent faith formation: *Choosing Church* (Carol

Lynch), *Effective practices for dynamic youth ministry* (Thomas East, et.al.), and *the Exemplary Youth Ministry Project (*Roland Martinson, Director, funded by the Lily Foundation 2003.

These essays describe best practices for adolescent faith formation drawn primarily from the three research projects. We also acknowledge consulting the research findings from the ten-year Youth Ministry and Spirituality Project (Mark Yaconelli) on contemplative youth ministry.

The best practices in adolescent faith formation described here are a summary of the findings of these studies I share them with the reader as a resource. For those with additional interest, I direct you to these studies which can be found online at *Http://www.faithformationlearningexchange.net*

In closing this discussion of faith formation, I draw your attention to the thoughts of John Roberto, the author of the above web site who makes the following observation concerning the best practices suggested in the study.

> *"Best practices…demonstrate that congregations can make a significant difference in the faith lives of young people. Even with the heightened sense of personal autonomy, even in these times, when believing and belonging means something individual, expressive and non-institutional. Religious traditions attract and hold teens in new and powerful ways. Teens tend to choose faith when they live in families (and communities) that talk the walk and walk the talk."* (*Best Practices in Adolescent Faith Formations,* Life long Faith Associates, Fall/Winter, 2007*)*

Seven best practices.

Seven "best Practices" are conceived in a manner so that each is set up with goals that can be measured, attained, and evaluated. Not all seven must be accomplished; they are interchangeable and can be addressed in any order.

These practices take on different aspects. Titled as "best practices" in the curriculum of the United Church of Christ, each approaches youth faith formation from the perspective of activities that involve teenagers. Teens will be involved in communities that strengthen acceptance and belonging, spiritual disciplines and contemplative practices, engaging teens in life ministries of service, respect for the way teens learn in contemporary society, and the interplay between socialization and religious development. Since this is a summary of the "practices" ministry of the UCC curriculum, the reader is directed to (copyright: United Church of Christ, 2012, Faith Practices is a licensed trademark of United Church Press.)

1. Two movements in adolescent faith formation need be generated at the same time – socialization and experience. Congregations that teach both the Christian way of life (socialization) and create conditions where teens feel they meet God tend to have more success keeping teens involved in the religious community where teens can practice their faith.
2. Creating a sense of belonging that ties them into the fabric of the congregation community.
3. Encourage spiritual discipline and contemplative practices. Teens are looking for how ideas are embodied; how faith impacts life when lived out by following Jesus' mandates.
4. Equip and engage teenagers to participate in the life, the ministries, and practices of the congregation. Seek ways to integrate youth fully in the life of the congregation.
5. Equip, nourish and, support parents in sharing faith with teenagers. Capitalize on the importance to teens of parental modeling of faith and religious practices.
6. Utilize a variety of models for teenage faith formation. There is no one perfect way to influence teen religious faith and practices.
7. Encourage learning activities that are experimental, image–rich, multisensory, and engaging. Begin with real life issues and connect with a life of faithfulness.

9

WHAT WORKS

Teaching confirmation may be a contact sport

"Good evening ladies and gentlemen and welcome to our annual Developing Spirituality Workshop. "A stately woman addresses the parents of the 2015 confirmation class gathered in the fellowship hall of the Springfield United Free and Open Church.

"Tonight we will be presenting some of the strategies we have developed to help kids listen up, pay attention, and grow strong spiritual bones in their emaciated, undernourished, and gaunt bodies. We call this the Wonders Never Cease Program for Spiritual Formation of Adolescents."

Parent's reaction is animated and enthusiastic. You can see the pumping of fists and hear the muttering of *"yes, yes"* above the din of the air conditioner and the clanging of pots and pans coming from the adjacent kitchen where the Women's Fellowship is preparing the evening refreshments.

"We begin with a power point presentation," the speaker announces as she fiddles with her computer and adjusts the volume on her microphone. Pictures appear on the screen. Visible is a group of fifteen junior high students, male and female, sitting bolt upright in a single row behind a long table. Duck type holds students' in their chairs. Their eyes emanate blank stares and are held open with Q-tips. Covering their mouths is more tape. Mr. Potato head large

plastic ears are stuck to the side of their heads, so they can hear better.

"These kids are about to receive their spiritual indoctrination," she announces and changes the image on the screen. *"It is meant to last a life time,"* she adds.

At precisely that moment, each student is directed by the drill sergeant dressed in a clergy collar to pick up a glass of white pasty-like substance labeled "divine milk," rip off the tape around their mouths, and consume the entire contents. They do as instructed. The lights come on and the screen goes blank. The leader begins speaking.

"The spiritual education of today's adolescents' calls for extreme measures," she states. *"Faith formation of kids is a crap shoot. This is just a sampling of ways we have come up with to assure success. Any questions?"*

Spiritual curiosity or creeping apostasy

It's no exaggeration. Faith formation is a crap shoot. That's the dilemma we face as Christian educators and parents. We desperately want our children reared in the same Christian faith we claim for ourselves, but research shows that this may or may not be a possibility. Smith and Denton, (*Soul Searching*) fortified by Kenda Dean, (*Almost Christian*) believe that the "faith of our fathers" as proclaimed by the present teen generation, is really an imitation of the authentic Christian faith. Teenaged Christian beliefs are basically dormant and without conviction. Unfortunately we have learned that following in the footsteps of the previous generation (their parents) may not contribute much toward building the teens "consequential faith." The parents' may be the problem. Their faith may be so simplistic that a naïve version may be the only faith they pass on to their children.

In our eagerness to nurture a Christian faith we look at the confirmation experience through rose colored glasses with an almost mystical wonder. We believe confirmation is some sort of charmed formula or magical inoculation that will render adolescents immune to creeping apostasy and fill them with spiritual curiosity. Our hopes and dreams belie reality; nothing like this ever happens. No single magic bullet has proven successful beyond all uncertainty.

All this makes confirmation a crab shoot as well. We plan diligently, we develop resources, we test out curriculums with control groups, we study the nature of adolescent brains, and still we wonder if anything gets through. Success is subjective; it depends on whom you ask.

Each local church retains something unique to their own tradition, something they feel is crucial to keeping their historical convention alive. For some, it's the notion of "we've always done it this way." They hold a stubborn inclination to sustain confirmation customs consistent through generations without changing a single artifact or ritual. Students are like empty pitchers just needing to be stuffed with knowledge to overflowing. Once saturated, their faith will be sufficient.

Not all congregations' approach confirmation in the same way. Some opt for more innovative means. They seek new paths to nurture an unchanging faith in a constantly changing environment; forever on the lookout for new curriculum material that will address adolescents emerged in the ways of the cyber world. Whole denominations have abandoned printed materials for downloadable internet designs that are updated momentarily.

Others congregations remain on the cusp. A little of both perspectives serve them well. Begin with denominational curricula and juxtapose contemporary theory when appropriate. All seek the same outcome - a means to nurture and enhance faith formation and to encourage adolescents to make lasting commitments.

Success is often illusive despite the preferred methods. Determining a measurement of success is often ambiguous and fleeting. It is impossible to glean a single standard or criteria to judge outcomes. For many congregations the emphasis is on retention - how many confirmands actually join the church and stay active. They use numbers to justify progress. Compare these statistics with the graduation rate - those who rarely return - and one has a measurement of success.

For others, it is more personal. Success is a subjective judgment. Testing is difficult, if not impossible. No external criteria exists, only a "feeling" one gets that the program touched the student's faith strings and influenced awareness of Christian practices. Nice feeling, but one never knows. In a student-centered, goal oriented world only the confirmand really knows.

Who knows what works?

Despite the abstruse nature of success in confirmation, it is still helpful to listen to those who are actually the leaders and planners- pastors, parents, mentors, and congregation members. Each provides judgment but in a different way and from a different perspective. The pastor, trained in theological conversation, is in a unique position to gauge the confirmand's ability to know and understand the language of faith. Parents and mentors are the "encouraging factors," they foster relationships and tend to mentoring with students. They provide reflection on the confirmand's growth and willingness to be an empathic and compassionate Christian. The congregation as a whole becomes the "welcoming committee." It is into their fraternity the confirmand will commit. They make judgments about participation. Taken together, these three groups (pastors, parents/mentors, congregations) provide significant insight into what is working and what is not in the confirmation education program.

No litmus test emerges that satisfactorily measures all aspects of confirmation education, but research and reports directly from those involved (pastors, teachers, congregation, and confirmands) does coalesce around a number of common denominators and persistent attitudes.

Some common denominators/attitudes.

Not everyone likes adolescents. They can be a challenge. Some pastors I spoke with openly admit to a distain for anyone under sixteen. Junior high is a difficult time in any teen's life; consumed by the fear of pimples, deathly afraid of girls, and still possessing a voice so high pitched it hurts the ears. You have to like what you are doing if you want to influence adolescents.

You were once an adolescent. You know how painful it can be. You don't want to go back there and they don't want you to become one of them. Don't be afraid to be an adult. Knowing how adolescents think, act, and behave gives you some clues on how best to relate to them. Promoting the adolescent's feeling of acceptance and belonging is not difficult. Here are some tips for building healthy adult relationship with adolescents, some common denominators indicative of all teens. As mentioned previously in the book, all these attributes also contribute to building a community and encouraging a sense of belonging.

1. *Show respect: Learn their names. Recognize each adolescent as an individual and don't play favorites.*
2. *Be patient: Building trust and rapport takes time. Take your cues from their timelines.*
3. *Establish clear boundaries: No need for you to be a best friend. Stay in your role as adult. Don't discuss your personal life.*
4. *Be consistent: Adolescents do best with regular structure. They are not good at too much "free time." Be consistent when implementing limits and tolerating behavior. Establish boundaries.*
5. *Listen: Pay attention and hear what they are saying even if you don't agree. Avoid giving too much advice.*
6. *Recognize they are growing up in a different era than you: Enough said.*
7. *Don't embarrass: Embarrassment is the worst debasement. Pull them aside for personal conversations when necessary.*
8. *Don't tell adolescents how they should feel: Invalidating their feelings and perspectives makes it unlikely they will share with you again.*
9. *Avoid blame: Even when the adolescent shares some responsibility for a problem, be careful about laying blame too quickly.*

Methods of instruction.

Finding points of identity and relevance are keys for nurturing faith in adolescents. Adults may point teens towards faith but teens must see for themselves the connections between faith and life. Abstract concepts remain elusive to the young mind. Teens are at a stage where they find it difficult to wrap their minds around theoretical thoughts. The key to enabling a teen to integrate faith with life is to connect a characteristic of God with a facet of the teen's world. For instance, the adolescents can best perceive trust in God as an extension of trust in a real person. If trust exists between the teen and others (parents, mentors, and friends), that trust is transferred easily to an abstract God. It is a process of moving the teen from known experience to the unknown; from life experience to spiritual experience and back again. How this is accomplished in the confirmation program varies, but to the extent that trust is the foundation of people to people relations it is also the foundation of the relationship between people and God. It is a relevant relationship and provides a learning experience.

Contrasting styles of teaching.

A variety of "models" are proposed with varying degrees of success. None are outstanding to the exclusion of all others. Which one you choose is a personal judgment.

1. **Pastor-led model:** This is the most traditional model. Pastors teach the catechism because the congregation believes they are the authorities and most knowledgeable. This is not always true.
2. **School model:** Congregations that have a weekday school program as part of their educational ministry incorporate confirmation as part of the curriculum. Sometimes the pastor is the teacher, but not always
3. **Youth group program model:** On occasion the youth group will be the context in which confirmation is taught. This model, by necessity, tends to be informal with lots of dialogue.

4. **Small group model.** There is continued experimentation with confirmation happening in small groups where give and take, dialogue, and discussion can be experienced in depth. Of the models, this is the most difficult to pull off. Just because a group has few members does not mean it practices "small group dynamics".
5. **The family model:** Parents take responsibility for teaching the tenets' of the Christian faith to their teenagers. While other models focus primarily on the church's role, this model leaves the decision making and the curriculum up to the parents.

The teaching and the teacher rank among the most powerful influences affecting confirmation experience. Where teaching is exemplary and methods relevant the odds for consequential faith formation increase. There exists some debate, however, about teaching approaches. Both are techniques employed by the principal teacher – the pastor to exclusion of the other models mentioned above. One is traditional – an authoritative teller of the traditional story and the other experiential – the sympathetic counselor concerned with drawing out the student's inner spiritual concerns and attitudes.

The traditional emphasis is on content. The teacher is an informed authority with the ability to transfer biblical, theological, and traditional content through lecture, instruction, or demonstration. Most pastors are consumed by their own theological knowledge and are anxious to pass this along to confirmands. Unfortunately, the language used is, for the most part, incomprehensible to teenagers. Teens cannot be expected to know and understand such words or phrases like "revelation" or "original sin" or "transubstantiation," or what a resurrection experience is all about. Yet, a theologically trained pastor cannot help but to infuse these concepts into the teaching of confirmands.

The pastor as counselor is radically different. The counselor role is to draw the student into self-discovery.

The focus is to enable the student to use decision making. The decisions are the foundation of a consequential faith.

But pastors have only the minimal obligatory education in counseling. They mean well, but do not have the acquired traits for professional counseling. Besides, it is a risky venture to enter into a counseling relationship with one teenager, much less a whole covey of teens.

There are problems with both methods. With a traditional approach, the teacher is often viewed as moralizing, a purveyor of the congregations ethical standards imposed on the confirmand. This invites rebelliousness by those not wishing to be "preached to." On the other hand, the self-discovery model relies on the discourse of adolescents who are uninformed, but expected to draw their own conclusions. Unfortunately, Christian beliefs are not democratically decided. So....despite that both are reported as "successes" both have inherent problems.

Both models working together appear to offer some hope. Knowing basic Christian tenets is essential, but the tradition might have more impact and clarification if the confirmand is encouraged to question it, analyze it, and dissect it before digesting it. Dialogue, I am convinced, is an appropriate form of learning, especially for the uninformed. Dialogue between the two methods encourages receptivity, especially for the adolescent brain that borders between concrete and abstract thinking; and is in need of seeing relevance as a condition for understanding. Allowing for discussion of information and concepts provided by the teacher encourages dialogue and discovery on the part of the student. A composite between these two models appears to be successful in capturing what interest there is among adolescents. Deriving this strategy is never easy; but strategies do exist and are often dependent upon other factors including, but not limited to the following:

Setting priorities.

Confirmation does not exist in a vacuum. If it is the only contact the adolescent has with the local congregation, chances are it will have little impact toward *"consequential"* faith formation. When confirmation programs prove influential it is because the congregation places a high priority on youth ministry. Where your treasure is, so also will be your heart. Throwing money toward youth ministry will probably produce results. Congregations that invest in educational programming for youth - church school, curriculum materials, youth ministry leadership, youth groups, youth facilities, and continual activities - tend to see more regular participation in the confirmation program. There is the "spill over" effect" or "trickle-down" theory at work here. Adolescents engaged and included in a community like the feeling of security and inclusion.It becomes a draw rather than an obstacle for their continued immersion. Like any persons, but especially for adolescents, when they recognize that someone thinks they are important, important enough to invest time, money, and resources, they respond whole-heartily to that initiative. Isolating the confirmation experience from the rest of the ongoing life of the congregation makes it feel like it is a once in a life-time inoculation; a hedge against apostasy that might better occur at a later stage in life. No one, especially the adolescent, looks forward expectantly to this experience.

What works? A research study

One exception to this, the only exception that an internet search could uncover, was an article in *Word and World*, (11/4, 1991 by Word & World, Luther Seminary, St. Paul, MN. page 382 Confirmation Programs in the Congregation: What Works? KENT L. JOHNSON). The author apparently was commissioned to find out "What works in confirmation programs in congregations". He undertook a brief and unscientific survey of asking local pastors to answer a variety of questions about confirmation programs. Specifically he wanted to know what works best from their experience. The results were a mixed bag of differing perspectives. Most of those he queried didn't even reply. Those who did presented an assortment of opinions from which the author, Kent Johnson, gleaned some common characteristics of perceived successful confirmation programs.

In the first instance, Johnson asked pastors to rank the "usefulness" of present confirmation programming in their congregations. He received varied responses that fell into certain categories often depending on the pastor's understanding of the question. Most pastors thought confirmation could be useful, but in its present state, it was not highly functional or successful.

When asked what makes confirmation instruction work, most pastors agreed on the following:

1. The stronger the congregational support the better the program.
2. Staff involvement needed to be committed and continual.
3. Congregational expectations needed to be high.

An interesting point of agreement among these pastors was the concept of integration. They all suggested that confirmation be an integrated part of a larger youth ministry program and not an isolated event at one specific time in a teen's life. By this, they meant that confirmation was not strictly academic. It needs to be experiential and relational, not just cognitive, if it is to make a significant and lasting impact upon teens. Confirmation needs to be integrated into the ongoing youth ministry throughout the teen years. A single year experience is not sufficient.

A third category of success oriented programs revolved around restarts and mentoring programs. Restarts are programs that duplicate themselves every few years. Most all pastors emphasized that such programs contribute toward the commitment of "disciples"; a vague, but stated purpose of most all confirmation programs. Mentors make a difference. They are the "connection" between the teen and the congregation. In short, those programs that appeared most successful were a result of congregational support of putting money where your mouth is.

Parent's participation.

Closely allied in importance to positive congregational attitudes toward youth ministry is the degree and intensity of parental support. Here we have somewhat of a dilemma. From the research of Smith and Denton (*Soul Searching*) and supported by Dean (*Almost Christian*), we learn that part of the reason why so many "Christian" adolescents have an overly simplistic understanding of their faith and religious practices is precisely because of the influence of their parents. This suggests a "hands-off" policy for parents. Yet, other research clearly shows that parental support and prodding of adolescents toward faith participation, particularly participation in the faith community, is of the highest priority and produces the greatest impact on faith formation. Sounds a little like "you're damned if you do and damned if you don't." Parents' beliefs passed on to their siblings may not represent the authentic tenets of the Christian faith, but parent's encouragement of their teens to participate in the Christian community is a positive step towards regenerating the teen's faith and beliefs. Pastors responding to inquiries consider parental support crucial, the more directed the support, the more impact it has on youth participation in confirmation.

A big difference exists, however, between asking for parental support and requiring it. Many congregations encourage it, but do not mandate it. As a result, there are different outcomes. For instance, under the rubric of "expectations," one Methodist congregation states that parents should "*ask their teenagers regularly about confirmation and engage in conversation about materials being studied, encourage completion of assignments, ...and bring teenager to worship, classes, and assignments.*" "Asking" and "encouraging" are not the same as mandating. Too much remains at the discretion of the parents, who will probably ignore these "suggestions" because of an already overcrowded schedule with priorities that lay elsewhere.

Mandating is a powerful tool, so long has the mandates carry some authority with them. One congregation offers the following: "*The participating parent or guardian is required, along with the student, to attend all outings and class sessions and do all class assignments.*" Unfortunately this congregation amends this mandate with the following; "*great effort will be taken in planning assignments and class meetings to accommodate family schedules.* Still they maintain that, *"regardless of the reason,...if a participating parent or guardian misses many of these events, they will be asked to drop out of the confirmation program."* Some strong language there, I only hope they mean it. The bottom line, however, is that confirmation does not exist in a vacuum. It relies upon support of the whole congregation, most especially, the parents.

Mentoring.

Mentoring makes a huge difference in the quality of the confirmation experience. Mentoring relationships take many variations, but always it is the pairing of one confirmand with one active, involved, and committed adult member of the congregation (like Mr. Black). Connecting is the mandate of mentoring; connecting a prospective member with an active member.

Religious formation and a consequential faith do not happen accidentally, according to Kenda Dean. They are learned behaviors. Over and over modeling is emphasized as a necessary tool leading toward faith practices. Choose mentors wisely.

Dr William Willimon adds to this discussion with the following:

> *"Most of us became Christian by looking over someone else's shoulders, emulating some admired older Christian, taking up a way of life that was made real and accessible through the witness of someone else. So, while books, films, and lectures could be used for confirmation class, they should only supplement the main task of putting young Christians in close proximity with older Christian mentors who invite these younger Christians to look over their shoulders as they both attempt to live as Christians."* (Christian Century, March 16, 1988, p.17 used by permission).

Mentoring especially helps youth as they go through challenging life transitions, including dealing with stressful changes at home, with peer groups, with school activities, and transitioning to adulthood. Close, healthy, supportive relationships between mentors and mentees that last for a significant portion of time (i.e., more than one year) are crucial for success. Without adequate mentors with enough devoted time to give, mentoring programs run the risk of harming young people who are paired with mentors ill-equipped to meet the mentees' needs. Where mentors are unprepared and lack skills to relate to youth; and where there is no emotional bond between the mentor and mentee, such relationships can prove harmful to youth.

Mentoring is an inter-generational program. Few components of an inter-generational program are as vital to success as strong personal relationships. But like any other relationship, success between you and your protégé won't just happen. It will take skill and hard work on both your parts to make your relationship grow.

Pastors and others using mentoring effectively with adolescent confirmands remind us of some key factors:

- Allow time for trust to build.
- Keep conversations confidential.
- Be consistent. Reliability fosters respect.
- Offer praise when appropriate.
- Respects mentee's choices.
- Don't be afraid to offer your own opinion.
- Be sensitive to feelings.

Trust is a two-way street. The mentee may want to "test" the mentor and there will be those times when you are suspicious about the mentee. Work it out and don't give in or give up. Experiment with trust. (From the work of the *Work Group for Community Health and Development*, University of Kansas, communityhealth.ku.edu/)

Choosing appropriate mentors takes some practice. Those who report on successful mentoring suggest that the confirmand and family indicate a person with whom they would feel comfortable. Make this choice known to the teacher who asks the prospective mentor and shares with that person the responsibilities. (If the teacher is the pastor, he/she can advise since he/she probably knows the person.)

Rarely, when asked, does a prospective mentor decline; rather they see it as an honor.

Retreats.

One youth leader remarked that "he would gladly trade 52 weekly Sunday school classes for one retreat." There is something unbelievably powerful when we take teens out of their normal environment and give them a chance to experience something new. The possibility exists, if not the reality, that kids who are incredibly busy with school, extra-curricular activities, and family obligations are able to slow down enough on a retreat to connect with God and their peers in a way they normally could not. Teenagers are busier than ever before. This makes it all the more important, if faith formation is to have any impact, to take students away from ordinary schedules and get them away, even if only for a week-end.

The environment for a retreat becomes important. Plan it for out of town away from parents. Because of the lack of intrusions and distractions, the retreat provides a time for teens to grapple with faith issues along with the many other issues that consume teen's time and energy. It is an opportunity for teens to discover faith and then to celebrate it in the context of their peers. The retreat setting, a time that concentrates on the relationship of teens with adults, enables authentic connections to be made that previously might have been very superficial.

Adults, who want to be approachable to teenagers, find the retreat setting to be an ideal opportunity. Adult mentors can talk with teens about faith issues because the teens "expect" such conversation to take place on a retreat. Here you have three days (weekend retreat) of uninterrupted time and ability to focus on the subject. No matter the theme, ceremonies, disclosures, and intense communication, group retreats serve to strengthen ties among participants.

Planning the retreat is the key to success. Give careful consideration to such aspects as place, time and date, structured and unstructured activities, and commitment from both teens and parents.

No matter the nature of the teen's faith, successful retreats share common elements. Foremost is the setting. Teenagers, you will discover, become different people when they are away from their normal settings – away from home and parents and siblings, away from the lure and temptation of shopping and video games and cell phones. Despite that their cell phones appear to be extension of themselves; clones of their personality, once they are abandoned, teenagers' exhibit tendencies of being real people. It is almost like they are glad to be relieved from having to check their cell phones five times each minute. To be someplace where these things can happen requires that a location be considered carefully. It needs to be a place where teens are required to stay overnight. Change the physical and psychological environment as necessary.

The structure for a teenage retreat matters. Draw a balance between planned activities and free time. It is my contention, after numerous failed retreat moments, that adolescents are not always good with lots of free time. This sounds counterintuitive, but it is true. Too much free time leads to boredom and boredom encourages teens to fill that time with destructive and unrelated activities. Free time becomes more creative when it is limited. When students know they have limited free time they are more apt to use it creatively.

If your teenagers have never been on a retreat, it may be difficult to convince them to try it. It is especially important to cast the vision of the retreat to parents. Start publishing the dates far in advance, allowing time to amend and adjust the plans if reaction is negative. It also encourages participants (teens and parents) to put it on a calendar early thus avoiding schedule conflicts.

Retreats often serve as catalysts for beginning a faith journey, particularly with suspicious teenagers. Research has shown that one of the most important factors influencing teens beginning a faith journey is the friends they meet at retreats. They are among other teens who are there for the same reason, hence the suspicious teen has ltttle to fear by exposing religious concerns, doubts and beliefs. He is among cohorts who probably have similar feelings and attitudes. In addition, adult mentors are present to deal with religious beliefs and practices that appear to be under scrutiny. It is interesting to note research has found that the most mentioned influence among teens becoming Christian was, believe it or not, a church retreat. (The Association of Youth Ministry Educators).

Addendums

INTRODUCTION

This section presents a variety of work book sections. Confirmation is nothing if it is not "hands on". Each of these sessions employs a teaching method I have found meaningful and attention grabbing for teenagers. If and when they must put the "rubber to the road" and actually talk about and get involved in their own faith formation, many of the activities in this section provide incentives and invite discovery.

The first section deals with the "troublesome teachings" of Jesus. Jesus' statements and mandates are often confusing. He raises more questions than he answers. Each of these activities suggests both scripture as well as a means for getting into its meaning. What are the implications for our time and in our place? They encourage dialogue between teacher and student as well as among students.

The sections are in the following order:

1 Troublesome teachings – Introduction.
2 God's System – Student worksheet – Addendum 1
3 Mixed Messages – Student worksheet - Addendum 2
4 Riches in Heaven – Student worksheet - Addendum 3
5 Promise Keepers (1) – Student and teacher worksheet - Addendum 4
6 Promise Keepers (2) – Student and teacher worksheet - Addendum 5

Later sections propose worksheets and activities (both student and leader) that encourage dialogue built around issues of faith formation.

Worksheet Creedal Thinking – Leaders guide – Addendum 6

Symbols, Their Meaning – Student Worksheet – Addendum 7

How Important Are Symbols? – Leader Guide – Addendum 8

Here We Stand – Confirmation Object Lessons – Addendum 9

Spiritual Heart Attacks – Student worksheet – Addendum 10

Losing your Livelihood –Teacher Guide – Addendum 11

Losing your Livelihood – Students worksheet – Addendum 12

Addendum 1

THE TROUBLESOME TEACHINGS OF JESUS - Introduction

Content: (for the instructor) The teachings of Jesus are not mere meaningless platitudes meant to console the anxious and placate the pious. They are as much about calls to action and changes in attitude as they are about spiritual harmony and maintaining the status quo. They inspire spirituality, but they also mandate implications and require consequences

What Jesus teaches matters; it matters that we live our faith as authentic and faithful despite that it is often taxing and a bit of a challenge. His teachings have implications and demand explicit responses. Most of his teachings raise more questions than provide answers. They inspire growth in faith and help reveal the mysteries of God. They shed light on the major issues and relationships confronting us in our time and in our place.

What matters to Jesus is often troubling to us. There are times when he appears to directly contradict the religious laws of his time. There are times when he refuses to answer a question and instead raises a new one. He speaks about loving enemies, turning the other cheek, eating with tax collectors, hanging around prostitutes, and forgiving the unforgivable. He even tells us the first will be last and the last will be first and if you want to save your life don't be afraid to lose it.

Why are these teachings so often troublesome? Because they ask us to think outside the box; they disturb our status quo. They are upsetting, problematic, and disturb our perceptions of how things ought to be.

It's not about Jesus; it's what Jesus is about that is the central focus of this series of study sessions. Drawing from some of the most troublesome teachings, we will examine both the content and the implications of such issues as how to love those who don't love you, why losing your life will enable you to save it, our fear of making and keeping commitments, how independence is grounded in dependence on God, and why saying what you mean is not always meaning what you say. Jesus has much to say about these human attributes, not so much to be pleasing and consoling, but rather to be challenging and stimulating.

In all these matters concerning human characteristics, teenagers are already involved. Much of their daily lives tend toward the confusing. They can take these matters in stride, and usually, with some exceptions, are able to put them in some perspective. They work them out.

The hope for this series of studies will be to cast a light on the implications of Jesus' ministry heretofore not fully understood or perhaps ignored outright because of its troublesome nature. Once recognized as a core of Jesus' teachings, it can only broaden and fulfill the serious student's faith formation.

Each of the studies follows the same pattern. It begins with a connection between the biblical narrative and life as we live it. It continues with a presentation of the text in the context of the broader biblical story surrounding it. The relevance of the story to issues and relationships that shape our lives is then the focus of the third section. We conclude with questions and activities that involve the student in discovering it's implication for our time and in our place.. Along the way are tidbits of information to enable the student to glean every bit of understanding possible from the text and the study. Dialogue is always encouraged

Five studies are proposed in the first series:

God's system: An examination of Jesus mandate to love those who don't love you.

Mixed messages: Saying what we mean and meaning what we say·

Riches in heaven: Unraveling the mystery of altruism.

Promise keepers 1: Counting the cost of commitments

Promise keepers 2: Making and keeping promises

Addendum 2

GOD'S SYSTEM

Where Is the Justice of Charity at Home?

Rebecca, my youngest daughter, and I were walking to school one day. She was wearing a brand new dress and felt proud of how she looked. As we walked side by side, just talking, a sudden downpour erupted unexpectedly. Rebecca's new dress got immediately soaked.

For no apparent reason that I thought she would understand, I blurted out, "The rain falls on the just and the unjust." Being a minister, bible quotes come naturally.

There was silence for a moment or two as we continued trudging toward her school through the rain. Suddenly without provocation, Rebecca thoughtfully mused, "Yea, I guess that's a good system."

Knowing how the system works.

I once sat in with a church mission committee while they discussed a request they had received from a local family. The wife had asked for some assistance paying a long overdue utility bill. Unless she came up with sixty-two fifty ($62.50) by the end of the week, her family faced the possibility of having their utilities cut off. It was late November. Her note claimed they were desperate and pleaded with the congregation for help.

There was heated discussion. The mission committee had enough money. They could afford to pay the utility bill. They acknowledged the bill was legitimate. Still, they labored long and hard. What should they do?

"Why doesn't the father have a job," one member asked?

"We're not sure why he doesn't," replied another member. "He says he was laid off."

"Why was he laid off," asked still another member? "Or was he fired?"

One other member was concerned with other sources for assistance. "Have they asked others for help with this bill? You know, sometimes these people get help from lots of different organizations for the same need. They know how to work the system."

It soon became clear to me that the committee members where laboring under a cloud of suspicion. They were searching long and hard for a reason to deny this request, to justify a refusal without feeling guilty. A considerable level of doubt, tempered by irrational fear, emerged from their deliberations. Was the request deserving? Had the family earned the right to be recipients of the church's charity? By the end of the meeting they were still not sure. (This story can be tempered to fit an adolescent age group)

Generosity tempered by suspicion (Reference to Matthew Ch. 5)

We have a powerful need to be generous, no doubt about it. We respond overwhelmingly, particularly as Christians, to those in need. We pay particular attention to people we know who are facing crisis, to our friends who are hurting and suffering. Indeed, Christians are charitable people, at least in theory. Why did this particular committee become so hindered by a nagging suspicion, a fear of those asking for assistance, a mistrust that perhaps they weren't yet deserving enough?

Nothing new here. It's the same suspicions that Jesus confronts in Matthew 5. Up on the hillside as Jesus sat talking with his friends and critics, he attempts to answer some of the questions and doubts plaguing the minds of those with him. They were wary of how his teachings flew in the face of traditions and expectations of how people regarded those who were different. For us, listening to these teachings of Jesus is like listening to one end of a telephone conversation. We know what Jesus says, but can only imagine the questions that come from his critics that elicit his responses. A proverbial "you know" or "you have been taught" precedes each of his questions to which Jesus then replies, "But I tell you." It's as if he implies that what you have previously learned or how you have always acted may have been acceptable "back then" but now it is a new day and you have to think in new ways.

> *"...for he makes his sun rise on the evil and on the good, and sends rain on the just and the unjust. For if you love those who love you, what reward have you?"* ...(Matthew 5:45-47 RSV)

Freely given, freely give

There appears to be strong obstacles in our way to responding to God's command of "freely given, freely give." God clearly distinguishes between good and evil deeds. People are not perfect, and sometimes, many times do some pretty rotten things to each other. There are those who act justly and those who do not. It is the unjust deeds that we do, and not who we are, that are subject to God's judgments. God hates sin but doesn't give up on the sinner.

Still that doesn't completely satisfy us. We want to take it one step further. We want to make a distinction between good and bad people, between the just and the unjust circumstance, between the deserving and the undeserving among us. We are not free enough to give in response to need alone. Instead we are restrained by the expectations of the giver and the circumstances of the given. Despite the severity of the need, it is the person as well as the need that must meet our approval.

A prayer for doing the sun thing

"The sun rises and the rain falls on
both the just and the unjust,
the compassionate and the merciless,
the forgiving and the retaliating,
the peacemakers and the warmongers.
You created it that way, holy mystery;
But we wish you hadn't.

So may we learn to live that way,
the way Jesus taught;
to offer life…to offer love…to all living beings.
non-judgmentally, unconditionally, unreservedly.
Teach us to do the sun thing;
and in that holy way, to let our light shine."

Author unknown

And what of justice, master?

"The rain falls upon the just and the unjust alike; a thing which would not happen if I were superintending the rain's affairs. No, I would rain silently and sweetly on the just, but if I caught a sample of the unjust outdoors I would drown him."

…Mark Twain

"The rain falls on the just and unjust fella. It falls harder on the just because the unjust has the just's umbrella."

… Ogden Nash

Is life fair?

When Rabbi Kushner wrote *When Bad Things Happen to Good People, (*Random House, 1981*)* it is reported that many folks wrote to him suggesting he write a sequel, *Why Good Things Happen to Bad People."* The sufferings of the righteous are not the only thorny theological problem (Book of Job). The prosperity of the wicked and unethical bothers people at least as much.

Why do selfish, dishonest people seem to get away with so much? If God can't protect the virtuous from illness, calamity, crisis, disaster, and other people's cruelty, couldn't God at least send some thunderbolts in the direction of the mean spirited? And if God is not sure who these people are, we can all suggest some names for God to consider. For instance, I can think of half-dozen well place funerals that might benefit society. But my candidates for eternity in hell are still very much alive and kicking, some prospering beyond my wildest dreams. At the same time, I can recall some decent, fine, upstanding good people whose backs are literally against the wall. It doesn't seem fair to me.

> *"Actually the same problem is as old as the Bible itself. Jeremiah, Habakkuk, and the writers of the Psalms often appear to be more concerned about the prosperity of the wicked than the sufferings of the good. Psalm 37 admonishes us not to be troubled about the fact that the wicked prosper in this world because their end is sure and they will "be cut off". That's all well and good, but what I'd like to know is when?"* ...Douglas F. Parsons, *Is Life Fair?* Quoted in John Mark Ministries website, *www.jmm.org.*

Criteria for choosing.

What Jesus calls into question is not our propensity for charity; it is our criteria for choosing.

> *"For if you love those who love you, what reward have you?"* ...(Matthew 5:46 RSV)

Should charity begin at home? Maybe not. Maybe that's the root of the problem. Home is more than a place; it's an attitude, a point of view, a bias. Home is where you feel accepted, welcomed, part of the family. It is where you belong. Home is filled with people you know and like, where you feel safe and secure. We protect the security of home by including some and excluding others. We invite some in and keep others at arm's length with feelings of suspicion and apprehension. When we build fences, we are aware of whom we are fencing in and whom we are fencing out.

When crisis arises in the home, our response is willingly given. There is no challenge to charity or limit to our generosity when it's for the home. We are "supposed" to care for those we already like.

The question posed by Jesus is different. Does this same attitude prevail outside the home, with people we don't know or don't like; people with different customs and different attitudes. It is here that we struggle with different sets of expectations of "deserving" that often become obstacles in our path toward generosity. We are confronted with a troubling teaching of Jesus. Consider the following obstacles:

Blame – If the problem or need is your fault, then you are responsible, not me. You must solve it. Blame takes precedence over need. To give freely is to expound your problem.

Fear - Is the person taking advantage of us? Are we being "milked" by con artists, by people without scruples, without legitimate needs other than the lack of incentive to help themselves? Is laziness the real culprit and will we be condoning this by giving arbitrarily?

Values – I don't understand these people. Their values and life-styles are so different and strange. I find it hard to be compassionate without questioning. If I give, will it mean I am endorsing their values?

It is to these conditions that Jesus addresses his disciples. Jesus responds to these quirks in our generosity with a challenge that reaches beyond the expected. The "system" we use to protect ourselves is often the same system that holds us prisoner. We are not free to act generous. Our suspicions and fears bind us. And so Jesus reminds us – you are too used to being like this, unable to give freely, but now you are free to be different, free to give from the heart unencumbered by fears or suspicions.

> *"And sends the rain on the just and on the unjust.... You, therefore, must be perfect, as your heavenly Father is perfect."*
>
> (Mt.5:45, 48 RSV)

Reading from the scriptures Matthew 5:43-6:4

These teachings come at the end of a long section of "sermons" in which Jesus appears to be contradicting many of the religious mandates set down by the religious establishment of his day. They bring into focus the relationship between spiritual and temporal life. Acts of religious practice can not be separated from acts of humanity.

Questions for your group discussion

- What is the difference between loving and liking? When Jesus says, "If you love only those who love you, what reward do you have?"(Matt.5:46 RSV) What is he saying? How do you explain that to your children?
- Jesus tells us that the "sun rises on the good and the evil." (Matt. 5:45 RSV) So how are you supposed to know who is good and who is evil? What criteria do you use to distinguish?
- Jesus asks you to "be perfect as your Father in heaven is perfect." What are the chances of that? How will you respond to this request?

For your thought and consideration.

If charity doesn't begin in the nice, familiar secure home setting, where does it begin? The mandates of Jesus in scripture text imply that charity, as expected by Jesus, needs to be unconditional; not dependent upon any circumstance other that the perceived need of the other. This might be too utopian for even the best of Christians.

- Think about your worst enemy, someone you despise, someone you feel has shown no redeemable qualities, someone who thoroughly irritates you. Now think about that person needing your help. What thoughts come to mind?
- Does charity begin at home? Justify your response. If not, where does charity begin?
- The concept of charity implied in the teaching of Jesus is unconditional. Is that possible? If you think there should be some conditions, what conditions would you impose? Who decides if these conditions are just?
- Terrorism appears to be a wholly unjust cause. How do you define terrorism? Are there any conditions when terrorism is just?
- When you are the giver of charity, are there any expectations laid upon you? Are there conditions you must meet in order to be a "giver?"

Addendum 3

MIXED MESSAGES

At the age of two, little David already knows the power of "no." Each time his parents ask him to do just about anything, he responds with a resounding "no." Mom and Dad expect this. They understand the terrible two's. Despite his tantrums, he usually concedes to their wishes without serious consequences. His "no" is not so insistent that it jeopardizes his relationship with his parents.

By the time David is an adolescent, "no" will still be an option for him, but uttered under different circumstances. His rebellion has become an outgrowth of his surging hormones, teenage independence, his disdain for authority, and his newly found freedom of choice. Despite his parent's frustration over his apparent lack of respect, this too will eventually pass as he grows and matures. Any damage to their relationship is repairable.

David grows up, well almost. Hopefully he never loses his desire for independence, but his propensity for pure insolence is muted by his growing awareness of the advantages of cooperation and his need to be accepted and to feel he belongs. He recognizes that selfish pride and rebellion get in harm's way when building personal relationships. David becomes painfully aware that mature people make judgments about each other's integrity based mostly on what one does, not on what one says he/she is going to do. Still, David encounters occasional discrepancies between what he says and what he does. These mixed messages affect his relationship with others. So also is his relationship to God altered.

Reading from the scriptures: Matthew 21:28-31

Always aware of our human tendencies and inclinations, Jesus draws distinctions between how we behave toward each other and how we respond to God. He knows we are a rebellious people. In this short story Jesus talks about two sons who react in contrasting fashion to a request from their father. By inference, the reaction of each son parallels the reaction we often make when asked to commit to God. We reply with mixed messages, ambiguous responses, and a lingering sense of rebellion that clouds our true intentions. Why is it that we cannot seem to say what we mean and mean what we say when it comes to making commitments to God or to each other?

> *"What do you think? A man had two sons; and he went to the first and said,*
> *'Son, go and work in the vineyard today.' And he answered, 'I will not'; but*
> *afterward he repented and went. And he went to the second son and said the same;*
> *and he answered, 'I go, sir,' but he did not go.*
> *Which of the two did the will of his father?"*
>
> (Matt. 21: 28-31 RSV)

The differing responses of each son characterize not only the confused responses we make to our faith commitments, but to our human obligations as well. Subjected to mixed messages, we often experience great difficulty deciphering between saying what we mean and meaning what we say. Despite that our actions speak louder than our words, we continually "shout out" a different message. Still, our actions are the basis upon which we judge all relationships – human and divine

An examination of the story of the two sons presents the Christian with many possibilities and teachable moments. The following are questions to review as you consider the circumstances of the text:

- How would you answer the question posed in the text, *"Which one did what his father wanted?"*
- Jesus is often asked questions about "who" (Who are my neighbors? Who did what the father wanted?). He usually responds by talking instead about "how"

(How do you act neighborly? How do you do what your father wants?). What is Jesus trying to tell us?

- What does Jesus mean when he says to the chief priests and leaders, *"You can be sure that tax collectors and prostitutes will get into the kingdom of God before you ever will."*
- What did the father want the sons to do? What is the spiritual significance of this encounter?

For your thought and consideration.

The story of these two sons provides a great jumping off point for the Christian educator to begin some "values clarification." The story is charged with insinuation and innuendo, providing much fodder for debate and consideration. It pits "righteous conduct" against "empty platitudes." It raises issues about intention, commitment, and integrity. It hits at the core of our values.

I suspect that Jesus intends for the story to call into question the hypocrites who claim allegiance to God with their words, but not with their actions. But, because he uses real people under real circumstances, the story also opens doors for examining integrity as a condition for making and maintaining human relationships. I suspect Jesus knew this already. He seems always to be drawing connections between how we treat each other and how we treat God. Since it is so difficult to keep commitments to each other, how much more difficult is it to keep commitments to God?

Some questions.

- Rebellion seems to be an attitude we can't shake regardless of our age or stage in life. It seems so easy for us to "sin," but so difficult to admit to doing so. Why do you feel people have such an easy conscious when making mistakes but find it so difficult to admit to them?
- Our mixed messages often hide our true intentions. Perhaps we deliberately intend to confuse because we want to hide something. What we say gives a first impression. What we do gives a lasting impression.

Talk about the time(s) you deliberately diverted your intentions by what you said that contradicted what you did.

- Talk about the time(s) when you knew the right thing to do but chose the "other" thing instead. Why did you choose differently? What were you hiding/thinking?
- When have you said "yes" but meant "no?" Explain your actions.
- Write an epitaph – a word or phrase by which you want people to remember you after you are gone.
- When you regret what you agreed to do but haven't done, what should you do?
- Discuss the difference between "who you are" and "whose you are."
- What do you look for when considering making new friends? How do you want new friends to judge you?
- Discuss ways you feel that God acts as a model for how you make and maintain relationships.

Addendum 4

RICHES IN HEAVEN

Unraveling the mystery of altruism

A woman was chatting with her next door neighbor. "I feel real good today. I started my day with an act of unselfish generosity. I gave a bum a five dollar bill."
"You gave a bum five dollars?" her friend replied."That's a lot of money to give away. What did your husband say?"
"Oh, he thought it was a good thing to do. He said thanks."

--author unknown

Jesus tells the story of a rich young man who comes to him seeking

the key to eternal life (Matthew 19:16-22 RSV). *"If you would enter life, keep the commandments."* Jesus replies.

"Which;" but what commandments, the young man inquires?

Jesus reminds the young man about obligations against stealing and committing adultery and making false accusations and forgetting to honor parents. *"These are among the most important,"* he says

"All these I have observed;" the young man responds. *"what do I still lack?"*

Jesus adds one more mandate that hits home with the rich young man. *"If you would be perfect, go, sell what you possess and give to the poor and you will have treasure in heaven; and come follow me."*

The young man appears perplexed and confused. He thought it would be easier. He figured he had met all the conditions for eternal life. He is seeking self-justification, perhaps a way to bolster his own self-esteem. Verification that one has met all the conditions for eternal life acts as a metaphor for self-righteousness.

The rich young man realizes immediately that he cannot meet the conditions Jesus sets forth, either willingly or unwillingly. Too much self-sacrifice is required. He goes away feeling sad or hurt or both. He is unable to abstain from his predisposition toward self-preservation above self-sacrifice. His instincts bar him from giving up possessions. To give them away makes for a very vulnerable existence, one that he can't imagine could be of any benefit to him regardless of what Jesus says. He struggles between rational self-interest and unbridled altruism. He has not yet discovered that having esteem for others is a precondition for self-esteem.

The challenge of altruism.

Ayn Rand has defined altruism in the following manner; *that man has no right to exist for his own sake, that service to others is the only justification for his existence, and that self-sacrifice is the highest moral duty, virtue, and value.* (The Lexicon) Altruism is more than mere generosity. It goes beyond sharing. It mandates that the interests and welfare of the other person always takes precedence over self-interests. Altruism holds that the other person's needs are a blank check; there is no limit placed on the demands of the giver.

The above is an extreme definition. Perhaps a more acceptable understanding of altruism might include the following characteristics. Altruism:

: is directed toward helping others.
: involves a high risk or sacrifice from the giver.
: is accomplished for no external reward.
: is voluntary.

Rand's extreme definition of altruism implies the other's concerns always take precedent over our own. This poses some interesting scenarios. For instance, when we are on an airplane the attendants instruct us to put on our own oxygen mask before helping other people. In my role as pastor/counselor, I have often advised people who take care of other people that they need to take care of themselves first, otherwise they won't be able to help others. This is taking precedent over the other. Are these exceptions or prerequisites to altruism?

Some have suggested that as we consider the place of altruism and generosity in the experience of human motivation we can place the consequent behavior in one of two categories:

> (1) I regard you as a means to an end. I will exploit you, manipulate you, or use you in any way that suits me. The end is my survival and satisfaction. I shun helping you unless there is benefit in it for me.
>
> (2) I regard you as an end in yourself. I will help you in ways that clearly benefit you without regard for my own benefit even to the point of risking myself.
>
> -- source - The Prisoner's Dilemma (Axelrod, 1984)

Altruism comes down hard on the side of cooperation and against competition. Cooperation indicates that concern for the other's welfare ends up being concern for your own as well. Competition, on the other hand, mandates one winner and one loser.

Losing your life will save it.

Most major religions, and we include here most philosophic systems (the Ethic of Reciprocity), have independently arrived at very similar conclusions. Perhaps the wording is a bit different but the intention is the same. Human to human relationships are best conducted from the perspective of "*do unto others as you would have them do unto you.*" (Matthew 7:12 RSV). We are introduced to this generous spirit that God requires in Jesus' Sermon on the Mount (Matthew 5).

- God blesses those people who are merciful; they will be treated with mercy.
- Love your enemies and pray for anyone who mistreats you.

- When someone slaps you on the right cheek, turn and let them slap you on the other cheek.
- When people ask you for something, give it to them.
- If someone sues you for your shirt, give up your coat as well.

At times, the generous spirit feels almost instinctive, something we do naturally and spontaneously. If we were to see a small child about to be hit by a passing Mack truck, we would like to think we would risk our life and jump in front of the truck if, by so doing, we would save the child. We would do it without calculation. It would be a spontaneous act, done immediately, and without reasoning. It is what we would want someone else to do for us.

At other times, the generosity is a forced act done in opposition to our better judgment. Generosity and altruism are latent acts in people. It may be more blessed to give than to receive, but the inclination does not come without hesitation and thoughtful reconsideration It is a need waiting and wanting to be expressed. It needs coaxing to mature. Like the rich young ruler we do not always immediately consider, nor do we always know, what is necessarily in the best interest of the other person..

A spiritual state of being.

A willingness, without hesitation, to take responsibility for the care of others always has a spiritual foundation. It is a spiritual state of being. In the absence of God, the strongest argument one can make for acting generous is that I like it or it feels good. There is no compelling reason why a person should love or care about another person, at least not to the extent that they would give up their own self-interest for the sake of the other person. Perhaps future gene theory will conclude that generosity and altruism have a DNA connection, but so far we know of none. There is more evidence that it is a learned behavior and one's spiritual foundation has much to do with that learning.

Generosity is proclaimed by God, taught by Jesus, and is a condition for faithfulness. When God proclaims, *"Truly I say to you, as you did it to one of the least of* these *my brethren, you did it to me."* (Matthew 25:40 RSV), we recognize that the way we treat other people is the way we treat God. We glorify God by caring about each other. Because God demonstrates consistently and Jesus teaches emphatically that altruism is to be pursued vigorously, that is ample evidence to assume that it is an important ingredient for spiritual maturity.

Reading from the scriptures.

Jesus spends a considerable amount of time and energy caring about other people. He takes responsibility for their wellbeing. In true altruistic fashion, he eventually gives his life for the sake of others. That's what we firmly believe. Jesus cares especially for people who are not supposed to matter - poor people, prostitutes, sick people, the deranged, and the lepers. Take a look now at some of the more difficult and challenging scriptures:

- Luke 6: 32-33: Jesus challenges his disciples to think about the meaning of generosity as an act of faithfulness in a very different context. If you love only those who love you, will God praise you for that? The idea that charity begins at home may be overrated. It's too easy, Jesus implies, to love and care about people you already like.
- What about those you don't like? How easy is it to care about them?
- What would motivate you to actually go out of your way to help someone you know you don't like?
- Matthew 5:43-47: Jesus proclaims that God sends the rain upon the deserving and the undeserving. How does this challenge our thoughts about giving only to those we deem deserving of our help? Who decides who are the deserving?
- Does Christian generosity have special considerations that must be met before we respond to someone in need?
- Jesus shakes us up a bit with the following. *"He who loves father or* mother *more than me is not worthy of me;*

and he who loves son or daughter more than me is not worthy of me." (Matthew 10:37 RSV). Is this a hard hitting indictment against family relationships or a question to ponder about Christian commitment at its core? Explain yourself. How would you respond to Jesus if he were to say this directly to you?

- Luke 10:25-37: (The Parable of the Good Samaritan). Jesus redirects our thoughts about generosity. Jesus is asked the question, Who is my neighbor? He never directly answers that question. Instead he redirects us to think about how, how we can act neighborly. Generosity appears to be devoid of the who and instead focus on the how.
- Does it make a difference to you who the person(s) is who asks for your help?
- Do you find that you respond to appeals of charitable organizations because you like them rather than because of the need they represent?
- How can you change your attitude about how, when, and where you will give?

Addendum 5

PROMISE KEEPERS - 1

Making and keeping commitments

"Human beings are animals that make promises."

--Fredrich Nietzsche

A commitment is a promise to do something. We are never immune to commitments. Making promises is as natural to our lifestyles as breathing. We make promises to do things and other people depend on us to follow through. We rely on the promises of other people

- We ride with a friend driving a car
- We place our paycheck in a bank
- We make a date with a girl/boyfriend for the school dance

Each is an act of trust in a commitment. We trust that persons will live up to the promises and commitments they make. We trust our money. We invest our funds and accept debts from others backed by the full confidence of the United States government.

Promises unsaid.

Some promises are unsaid; not spoken, but promises nonetheless. We rely on them even without asking. They may not be written or sometimes even stated, but they are assumed to be as strong commitments as those are in a written contract.

- Children depend on their parents for commitments of nurture.
- Friends depend on commitments of confidence from each other.

- Spouses depend on commitments of respect, obligation and love promised to each other.

It is difficult to imagine any relationship between individuals or between nations of people which does not survive and thrive on making and maintaining commitments.

Analysis of commitments.

Promise making seems simple, but it can be fraught with snares and traps. Conflicts arise with those who don't deliver on commitments. We offend others when we don't deliver on our promises. Even with the best of intentions, we probably fail as often as we succeed in keeping our promises.

Some have suggested that making a promise does not comprise a valid commitment until the other person accepts the promise. Commitment making always involves two or more parties; there must be an offer made by one party and accepted by the other. It is always a "process"; a process of offering to do something, having the offer accepted, and then acknowledging that the "conditions of satisfaction" have been met. It's similar to a contract.

Not all promises turn into commitments. They often disintegrate somewhere between the making and the keeping. Sometimes we promise to do something that feels right and we proceed with the best of intentions, but we are not fully aware of all the consequences. The task may prove overwhelming or impossible to complete and we have to abandon the promise. There are always costs to commitments. We fail to count the costs for which we are responsible only to find out the costs are more than we can bear.

Counting the costs of commitments.

Consider the following statements about the "costs" of commitments and how easily they can be fraught with difficulty:

> *"If you develop a reputation for not meeting commitments you can be sure that the commitments that have been made to you will not be kept either. The reasoning is simple. The*

other person will adopt your attitude and consider it of no consequence by doing it all the time. So it is entirely in your hands – if you want others to keep the promises they made to you, it is essential that you keep the promises that you make to others."

...Internet Blog

"Fear of commitment is really about fear of rejection. If you don't commit, you don't feel committed. If you don't feel committed, then you can't be rejected. Is that why it's easier to have many superficial relationships than one serious, committed one? It's like putting all your eggs in one basket, or worse, having one egg. If it doesn't hatch, then you feel truly rejected."

...Internet chat room conversation.

"For which of you, desiring to build a tower, does not first sit down and count the cost, whether he has enough to complete it? Otherwise, when he has laid a foundation, and is not able to finish, all who see it begin to mock him, saying, 'This man began to build and was not able to finish."

(Luke 14: 28-30 RSV)

The costs and joys of commitments.

Commitments have the potential to turn into long lasting relationships even when not intended. As such, they often bring out our anxieties and fears. We prefer options and choices of shorter duration. Commitments demand accountability and responsibility over a longer period of time. That can prove to be scary.

Jesus never concealed the fact that his understanding of faith in God included a demand as well as an offer. The demand was as total as the offer was free. When he offered people a relationship with God, he also demanded their obedience and faithfulness over a long period of time.

One denominational Statement of Faith includes the following; "*He calls us into his church to accept the cost and joy of discipleship.*" (United Church of Christ, used by permission)

- What do you think is meant by the "cost" and "joy" of discipleship?
- How is accepting these costs and joys like making a commitment?

Reading from the scriptures. Mark 8:31-36

In this text, Jesus puts us to the test of real commitment. Faithfulness does not come easy and involves a commitment. He is almost daring us by suggesting if we are not willing to make the ultimate commitment – following Jesus, then don't make any commitments at all.

- The United States Declaration of Independence encourages the "pursuit of happiness." The gospels of Jesus encourage the pursuit of service. What do you see as the difference?
- Jesus sounds a bit annoyed or angry. At what is he angry?
- The text speaks of "saving" and "losing" your life. To what is it referring?
- To the question of Jesus, *"Does a person gain anything if he wins the world but loses his life"*, how would you answer him?

For your thought and consideration.

Some social commentators of our day have observed that today's American citizens live in fear of commitment.

> *"Contemporary society offers few highs and lows. People seem to be seeking pleasure and beauty, but they find mediocrity. They seem to want challenges but do not find any intellectual heights to scale or causes noble enough to champion.*
>
> *Surely the dullness of today's society reflects a lack of commitment. Few people are inspired to make the effort required to work to make their world a better place. We have no ideals, no goals that we are willing to commit our lives to achieving."*
>
> ...Steve Moore.

- What commitments do you fear making the most?
- What is your response to Mr. Moore's analysis?
- Identify a couple of persons you admire for their sense of commitment.
- What qualities or characteristics do you think makes them admirable? What keeps them going?

Some people have observed a wishy-washy attitude creeping into our churches. One frustrated layperson recently observed:

> *"My community service club asks more of me than my church. They fine me if I miss a meeting and give me a job whether I ask for it or not. My church, on the other hand, is paranoid about asking people to do anything. My pastor asked me to chair a certain work area but quickly added that it wouldn't require much effort."*
>
> (Anonymous quote from www.valleymorningstar.com.)

- Do you feel over or under committed?
- How do you decide what is important to commit yourself to? What criteria do you use?
- How strong is your commitment to your church community? Do you feel over used or not used enough?

Addendum 6

PROMISE KEEPERS –2

Genesis 6:5 – 9:17

Prayer. *We open ourselves to you lord. We ask that your word might break through today as an inspiration for us to learn about you.*

Bible story summary (Genesis 6:5-9:17). God's heart is filled with pain as God surveys the wickedness of humankind. Reluctantly, God declares that the created world should be washed away and creation started over again. God assigns Noah, a righteous man, to build an ark and include two of all species for preservation. Rain pours down and blots out all creation, save for the ark. God remembers Noah and the waters recede. Noah, his family, and his animal menagerie reach dry ground. God establishes a covenant with Noah to withhold further destruction forever.

Supplies.

- Copy of a marriage vow for each person. (ask pastor)
- Pencils or magic markers.
- Bibles RSV.
- CD music player

Hearing and sharing.

Ask the pastor for a copy of traditional marriage vows.

Begin by passing to each participant copies of the marriage vows. A volunteer reads the vows aloud. Consider the following:

- What promises are stated in the vows?
- Are these promises difficult to maintain for a life time?
- When can a promise be nullified, if ever?

Allow discussion about the vows but don't provide answers or conclusions

Prayer. *Lord, our commitments and promises are often difficult to keep. But we are only human. Your promises, Lord, we can always count on and we are grateful.*

Hear the bible story.

The story of Noah and his ark has become so familiar it hardly needs retelling. The implications of the story, however, are far reaching, profound, and touch many aspects of the relationship between humans and God. Three aspects of the story need special consideration. Each section is heard in turn. The questions or activities following the reading are meant to help "digest" the theme/story intended in that section.

1. God is not pleased with the behavior of people on earth. They don't care for one another, for the land, nor do they care about God. Pain fills God's heart. God decides to wipe away all traces of living things on earth save for Noah, his family, and a representation of animal life. Read Genesis 6:5-8 and consider the following:
   - Sin abounds in God's creation. What bothers God the most in Noah's time? What bothers God in our time?
   - *"Noah finds favor in the sight of God"* (Gen. 6:8 RSV). What do you suppose constitutes Noah's righteousness?

2. The waters recede and Noah alights from the ark. Noah shows gratitude to God with a burnt offering on a hastily constructed altar. In turn, God blesses Noah and his family and mandates that they "be fruitful and multiply, and fill the earth" (Gen. 9:1 RSV). Read Genesis 8:20 – 9:1 and consider the following:
   - Is gratitude an act of dependency?
   - Do we live lives independent of God?

- How does our dependence on God provide for our independency?
- Read or sing the words of the hymn *God of our Fathers.* Words by Daniel C. Roberts

3. God establishes a covenant with Noah and his sons in which God promises never again to destroy the earth with floods and that life on earth will flourish and prosper. God sets in the sky a "bow" as a symbol and reminder of this promise. Read Genesis 9:8-17 and consider the following:

    - An evolving story. The first participant states aloud the following: *After the flood waters receded, this is the history of humankind from Noah to Obama…* Each participant adds to the story in portions until all have shared.

Reflect on the story.

- I wonder how Noah reacted when first learning the earth would be destroyed? I wonder about Noah's reaction upon being considered a righteous man in God's sight?
- What prayers might Noah have said when asked by God to build an ark? Were they prayers of gratitude?
- Considerate God's mandate that Noah and his family *"be fruitful and multiply and fill the earth"* (9:1 RSV). In light of the condition of our contemporary world, was it a good mandate? How has it turned out, well or maybe not so well?
- God said that the *"fear and dread"* of Noah will rest on all living things (Gen. 9:2 RSV). What do you suppose God meant? Do we live with any "fear or dread" today?

Connect to the story:

Beyond the story line of this narrative, there evolve particular themes that illuminate the relationship between God and his creation. God provides a sense of hopefulness in the midst of disaster. Despite the human tendency toward "corrupt ways," God is forgiving and sustains life. God's covenant with his creation is unilateral and unconditional. The following questions and activities are meant to highlight these themes: Choose one or all.

- Respond to the following quote. *"My community service club asks more of me than my church.* My mother-in-law Gene lived a very independent life until the day we found her on the ground in her backyard. She suffered a stroke. We moved her to an assisted living facility, but she became an unhappy camper. All the "assistance" bothered her. It made her feel, well…too dependent. Discuss: Are we ever truly independent persons? How dependent are we upon the promises of God? Which promises of God help us become/feel truly independent?

Respond to the story.

Guided meditation. A volunteer reads the guided meditation, pausing between lines for silent reflection.

Take a deep breath let it out slowly and name silently one sin for which you wish forgiveness. (Pause)

Think deeply about the condition of our world and offer up a silent prayer for its healing. (Pause)

Meditate upon why God thought Noah a righteous person. (Pause)

Consider what you can do this week that will promote justice or peace or care for the environment. (Pause)

Open your eyes. Offer a word of encouragement to the persons sitting next to you.

Supplies. None

- **Worship.** The bible says that Noah, acting out of gratitude for his salvation from the flood, offers up a burnt offering on an altar and the *"Lord smelled the pleasing odor"* (Gen. 8:21 RSV). Create a small symbolic altar (table with two candles) and ask teens to draw items on paper that might suggest a smell pleasing to God or use other symbols of things appropriate to give in gratitude for God's promises. Place items on altar.

Sing together the hymn, *We Gather Together to Ask the Lord's Blessing.*

Supplies. paper, crayons, magic markers, hymnal, table, two candles with holders.

- **Stewardship.** Genesis 9:1-6 implies that humankind has been given stewardship over the "new creation" after the flood. Plan a walk in a local park or open field with emphasis upon discovering forms of life difficult to see (bugs, ants, tiny grasses, geckos, etc.) Discuss our responsibility to these creatures beyond crushing, killing, or exterminating them. For teens, point out unseen killers such as pesticides, fertilizer runoff, and explain their proper use.

  Supplies. Magnifying glass, bug box.

- **God's Promises.** The promise God makes to Noah is one among many recorded in the Old Testament (see Genesis 12:3). Divide into three groups. Group one lists promises we depend upon family and friends to keep. Group two lists promises we depend upon the government to keep. Group three lists promise we depend upon God to keep. Ask each group to report.

Discuss.

- How can a promise turn into a commitment?
- What commitments do we fear making the most?
- How do we decide what is important to commit to?

Supplies. Paper and pencils.

Analyze biblical time. There appears to be confusion over how long Noah and his family survived on the ark. Using information gleaned from Genesis 7 and 8, attempt to draw a time line and come to some conclusions about how much time was spent on the ark. Discuss: From your mathematics, does the story appear more allegorical than factual? How do you explain this phenomenon to a teen?

Supplies: RSV Bibles, paper and pencils, small calculator

A rainbow of promises. On a large piece of poster board draw a rainbow and tape it to the wall. Have both teens and adults, if present, color it. Each person marks a spot along the rainbow with a word or symbol that depicts the most significant promise they feel God has made to them. Consider the following and encourage teen's responses.

- Are there similarities in responses?
- Are some promises more important than others?

Supplies. Poster board, colored magic markers, tape.

Ending and sending.

Prayer. *God, who promises to never leave us, who creates every living thing, who sustains life abundantly, be with each of us until we are together again in your name. Amen.*

Pondering. The narrative of Noah and the great flood is as much about hope as it is about destruction. It is a story of how God sustains life despite that humans seem caught up in sin. It is a story of God's salvation, a theme taken up by Jesus in the Gospels. Consider how the theme of salvation in the Old Testament is similar or different from the theme of salvation in the Gospels.

Addendum 7

TEACHING CREEDS TO TEENS

Saying what you mean and meaning what you say

(Note: The content of this worksheet is derived from material presented in previous chapters of the book.)

"In an age when accepted wisdom changes momentarily,
it feels strange to claim
some truths are so critical they bear repeating for centuries"

--Luke T. Johnson

What are creeds and what do they do?

On any given Sunday, millions of Christians recite the words to one creed or another routinely as part of their worship experience – the Nicene Creed, the Apostles Creed, or a denominational Statement of Faith. Sitting next to their parents are children with blank stares on their faces. They have no clue what a creed is and the words that resound feel similar to a foreign language. I wonder what they think about when they hear such phrases as *"judging the quick and the dead"* (Apostles Creed) or the tongue twister, *"one holy catholic and apostolic church"* (Nicene Creed)? No one takes offense at the words nor can they explain them particularly well. Instead they respond, "It's always been a part of my worship. I miss it when they are not included."

Creeds have been around for centuries. They have become, by repetition and tradition, an integral part of worship. Creeds were originally designed to help us process, define, and symbolize our faith. The words they use are easily memorized. The word creed comes from the Latin root meaning "I believe." Creeds are meant to define boundaries within which a group of people operate. While a creed is a rule in one sense, it is better defined as a fence dividing the preferred from the not-preferred. For the early Christian church, this meant that creeds originated often in response to some real or imagined heresy. Creeds are not intended to be infallible, but flexible, changing and developing over time to reflect the teachings of the faith in specific times and under specific circumstances.

> *"A creed, or Rule of Faith, or Symbol is a confession of faith for public use, or a form of words setting forth with authority certain articles of belief, which regarded by the framers as necessary for salvation, or at least for the well-being of the Christian church."* ... Phillip Schaff, *The Creeds of Christendom*, originally published by Harper and Brothers, 1877*)*

Often challenged by those addicted to the scientific method, creeds proclaim a faith that doesn't distort the real world, but rather illuminates reality from a different perspective. Creeds testify to the truth of faith as experienced by the believer. They describe what we believe about God and about our faith as we encounter these concepts in life circumstances.

- Creeds are statements of belief that matter. You can not hold a belief that something is true without admitting the belief matters. Stating the same belief as a creed affirms the belief makes a significance difference to you.
- Creeds don't exhaust the meaning of faith; they enhance it. Creeds are inclusive, not exclusive of the truth. Others may perceive the truth from a different perspective.
- Creeds are testimonies, not tests. Creeds are public avowals of religious experience intended to be helpful in describing a common faith
- Creeds don't create faith; they support it. Only a person who believes can express that faith as a creed.

Creeds are making a comeback, even in denominations that have previously balked at them. Many younger Christians who are discovering the Christian heritage, prefer to be connected to a larger and older tradition than merely the recent era. Creeds can connect believers to both past and present believers and provide a foundation for faith formation for those who experience confusion.

> *When parents ask the question, having been brought up with reciting the creeds, "How is my child going to learn the Apostles Creed?"they are asking a deeper question. It is a question of faith perspectivesin general "What do we believe, and how can we transmit this to the next generation."*

Goal for the session.

Learners will examine the tenets of Christian faith by constructing statements of belief, dissecting Christian creeds, and participating in dialogue about their faith practices.

Preparing for the session.

Leader will need –

- Half sheets of Paper (see below) with words friends, family, education, and God printed on it
- 3X5 cards with "beliefs and practices" words. (see section below)
- Newsprint or poster board
- Magic marker
- Pencils or pens.

Review the content of this student worksheet. Become familiar with the Apostles Creed, the Nicene Creed and some denominational statements of faith. (The web site *www.creeds.net* provides access to the words of most creeds and denominational statements of faith.)

GATHERING. (10 minutes)

Testifying, not testing.

Refer students to the section "testifying to the truth" below." Have one student read, while others follow along.

Following the reading discuss the questions:

Testifying to the truth. (Read out loud)

One day John was asked to go to the local Stop and Shop to get a gallon of milk. As he was about to enter the store, he was nearly bowled over by a person exiting. He was in a great hurry.

When John entered the store, the clerk told him he was just robbed by the person leaving. Did John recognize him?

John thought for a moment and then realized, yes he did. It was Bill Williams. Later that afternoon, the police called John to the police station to testify to what he saw. The officer asked him, "Are you sure it was Bill Williams?" Bill was then arrested.

About a week later, John read in the newspaper that a man named Hank Schneider confessed.

- Did John tell the truth when he accused Billy of the robbery?
- What determines what the truth is and what is not?
- Have you ever experienced something as "true" only to find out it wasn't?
- Are there some things you believe that are not true?

Teaching tip. Right answers are not important. To encourage faith articulation, dialogue between students and leader is important. Testifying is telling the truth as you experienced it. Emphasize that the truth is often expressed as "true" from your perspective. Untruth is saying something you already know is false.. A creed is a testimony to the truth of faith as you experience it.

Opening. (5 minutes) Focus on scripture.

Share the scripture reading from Luke 24:13-27 paraphrased

Exploring. (20 minutes)

1. Beliefs and practices. Statements of Beliefs.

Prepare half sheets of paper with the following words written across the top. What I believe about...friends... family...education...God. Title the page "Statements of Belief." Ask each student to write in the space under each of the following categories words or phrases that describe their beliefs about (1) friends, (2) family, and (3) education. Share responses (Teacher tip: encourage each student to defend the position. Play devil's advocate by suggesting that friends are not important, family makes little difference, and education matters little) Finally, ask them to write words or phrases about God. Share these statements with group.

2. More beliefs and practices.

Using a stack of 3X5 cards, write one of the following phrases on each of the cards. Place the cards in a basket or small box.

- It's not a religion, it's a relationship.
- God is a mystery.
- God always answers prayer.
- What happens is a miracle.
- Lord willing.
- I'll pray for you.
- Have you found Jesus?
- Thank you Jesus.
- Do you know where you are going after you die?
- Jesus loves you.
- He is risen.
- We're in the end time.
- Hate the sin, love the sinner.
- What's God doing in your life?
- I believe this because the bible says so.
- God is in control.
- I'm not a racist, but…
- Amen.
- All you need to get into heaven is ask Jesus into your heart.

On a sheet of newsprint, write four column headings. (1) Very important. (2) Not very important. (3) Not true. (4) I have no idea what this means. Explain to the students in your own words: *The box contains cards with religious phrases on them which you have probably heard before. Your task is to select one card from the box and tape it on the news print under the column where you think it best fits as a part of your understanding of faith.* Have each student draw a card. Tape it on the newsprint and return to the end of the line. Continue until all cards have been placed.

Discuss and dialogue with the group about the placement of each card. Encourage students to defend their choice of category for each statement, asking why they choose it as important or not important. Give explanations for those cards placed in the "I have no idea" column.

Responding (10 minutes) Used to Thinks/Now I Thinks

Prepare a work page for each student with two even columns. At top of first column write "used to think." At top of second column, "write "now I think."

Refer students to work page entitled "Used to thinks/ Now I thinks" Ask each student to take a few moments to write down words or phrases they "used to think" about God when they were children. In the second column ask them to write words or phrases they might use "now I think" about God. Spend a few closing minutes reminding them how they have grown in their image of God by the way they articulate how they "now think about God"

Closing (5 minutes) Luke 24 (portions)

Have group form a circle while one participant reads the following verses.

> *"Then he said to them. 'O foolish men, and slow of heart to believe all that the prophets have spoken...And beginning with Moses and all the prophets, he interpreted to them in all the scriptures the things concerning himself."* (Luke 24:25, 27 RSV)

- Ask each participant in turn to say one thing they believe about God or Jesus they might have learned during the past hour.

Alternative teaching activities. Dissecting a creed. Direct the students to read one of the traditional creeds (preferably the Nicene or Apostles creed) and underline any parts that are troubling or they find make little sense. As homework, ask them to find an adult member of their congregation to whom they can ask for an explanation of the troubling section in language. In their own words, students will write the explanation and share it with the class.

Scavenger hunt. Prepare a number of questions about symbols in the sanctuary of your church. Give each student the list of questions and a time limit to discover the symbols. Survey your sanctuary for appropriate symbols to use. Suggestions:

- Where is a cross located?
- Where is an alter?
- Where is a pulpit?
- How many pews in the sanctuary?
- Where is the baptismal fount?
- What symbols are on the baptismal fount?
- Where can you find the letters IHS?
- What pictures are on the stained glass windows?
- What carvings are on the pews' ends?

Discuss with students the meaning of each symbol and how it reflects the "creeds" of Christian faith.

Credible/ Incredible.

Write the words "incredible" and "credible" on newsprint.

Ask the group for the meaning of each word and write responses under the word. Introduce the word "creed," suggesting it means a statement of what you believe. Ask the group for any and all examples of where creeds exist they can think of. Examples: U.S. Constitution, athletic teams mottos, people believing in aliens, ghosts, political candidates.

Addendum 8

SYMBOLS TEACH FAITH FORMATION

(Note: Material for this workshop excerpted from previous chapters of the book)

Introduction.

The voice on the other end of the phone was pleasant, almost sweet. Clearly her accent gave her away. I could tell immediately she was from Alabama.

"Hi there, Ya'll doing okay today?"

She waited for my reply.

"Just fine," I replied. "And how are you?"

"My name is Dee Dee," she told me, "and I'm calling from the Miraculous Gospel Tee Shirt Ministry. We're located in Alabama. Are you the pastor?"

I assured her that I was but suspected she would keep talking even if I wasn't the pastor.

"I just know your youth group is itching to witness for Jesus," she informed me. "I want to help you. We think we have just the right symbol for them. It's a tee shirt made of authentic one hundred percent old Southern cotton and comes in a variety of colors. Most important," she continued, "it has printed in bold letters 'WE WORK FOR JESUS' right on the front. You can have the name of your church emblazoned on the back at no extra charge. Doesn't that sound like something your youth would feel proud to wear?" She seemed pleased with herself.

"They only cost $12.99 each or in lots of ten they are only $100.00 per box. How many would you like us to send you?"

"None," I said. I tried to end the conversation quickly,

but she would have none of that. She persisted on lauding the value of tee shirts as witnessing for Jesus.

"Why wouldn't you want your youth to show how much they love Jesus?" she insisted. "Teen tee shirts tell the world how much they care."

"Thanks, but we are not interested," I repeated several times and then hung up.

The importance of being a symbol.

Symbols are everywhere. Symbols are powerful. Symbols can persuade, they can convey, and they can motivate. They have the power to organize a crowd of miscellaneous people into a smoothly operating community bent on a single purpose. Some people have proclaimed that symbols are the natural speech of the soul, a language older and more universal that words.

Symbols may appear as only matter, but they "matter" a great deal. They can be transcendental. They can be inspiring. They capture the essence and meaning of experience. Symbols convey beauty, truth, and unravel the mystery of God.

The value of symbols and symbolic communication lies in the ability to touch human imagination and intuition and create a sense of awe and wonder, to instill a sense of beauty, and thus aid in the recovery of the mystery of the transcendent.

For generations, symbols– the cross, the fish, and the star - have been of immense importance to the Christian faith and its faithful followers. For the uninitiated, the bread and wine of the Eucharist may be only common elements. In reality, for the Christian they are the life blood and body of the very Jesus. Symbols such as these contain the power and dignity that transforms. The sanctified symbol takes on the very nature of that to which it bears witness. Christ is present in the bread and wine of the communion. The Holy Spirit is present in the baptism. The empty cross becomes a reality in the Easter resurrection celebration. The Christian father, Ephraim was keenly aware of the potency of symbolism when he wrote many years ago:

"In every place you look His symbol is there,
and when you read, you find His types.
By Him were created all creatures,
and He engraved His symbols His possessions,
when He created the world."

Religious symbolism is the use of signs and emblems to teach and recall religious truth and experience. Symbolism often succeeds in communicating where words fail. When taken together, symbols can sometimes make spiritual truth exceptionally evident. Symbols are always more than mere substitutes for the "real thing." They can serve as metaphors; they open up the meaning of the event toward which they point. Symbols illustrate that for which they stand.

Universal Christian symbols. Certain characteristics are unique to religious symbols:

- Image usually biblically based
- Conveys an essential biblical truth or teaching
- Generally a long tradition in church history
- Wide geographically recognition.
- Minimal code needed to unpack the image

(Adapted from *Symbols and the Christian Faith* www.wheaton.edu.)

Christian kitsch, holy hardware or Jesus junk?

Not all symbols that claim authority or credibility are authentic. Sociologists point out that we need to be aware of symbols that may not bear the true nature of that which they claim to represent. In any culture, including our contemporary society, religious symbolism can easily fall prey to distortion. It has its own way of becoming hollow.

It becomes increasingly difficult to determine the motivation for the use of symbols by unsuspecting Christians. The display of crosses, fishes, doves, scripture, and caricatures of Jesus are affixed to just about anything that sells. The question can ultimately be raised; does the use of Christian symbols become corrupted when it is used for a purpose other than representing the truth revealed through the ministry of Christ? Is wearing a tee shirt bearing the words "*We Work for Jesus*" sufficient as a demonstration of a vital commitment to Jesus or is it a substitute for authentic ministry?

Trinkets or trash?

Walk into any store advertising itself as a Christian bookstore and a plethora of stuff aimed at enticing the contemporary Christian will surely confront you. Within a cash register's tape length from the door, the merchandizing begins. Alongside the critical bible commentaries, bible translations, and musical CD's sits chewing gum wrapped in scripture paper, bible text adorning ornamental vases and statues, tiny red and white life savers announcing "Jesus Saves," and assorted bric-a-brac that asks the question "*What Would Jesus Do*?" Devices and objects with no apparent religious or moral nature are given sacred significance by imprinting upon them scriptural references and Christian symbols.

Some have questioned the conversion of the amoral to the spiritual. What is communicated? What message is conveyed by the wearer of shoe laces imprinted with "*Jesus Makes Me Happy*" on the left shoe and "*Jesus Knows What's Right*" on the right shoe? Marjorie Cooper, marketing professor at Baylor University in Texas has stated in an internet blog, "*I think that, to some extent, we're trying to peddle a popularized God in sound-bite mentality so that he's palatable for the masses. But God has never presented Himself that way. This is our idea.*"

Goal for the session.

Students will explore and experience symbols as a means for understanding the meaning of Christian beliefs.

Preparing for the session – Leader will need:

- RSV bible
- Wedding Ring
- Note paper and pencils for each student
- Prepared scavenger hunt lists (See activity for details)
- Access to Church sanctuary

- Lists of religious symbols (See Exploring section – Sanctuary Scavenger Hunt).
- 2 bells or whistles or other noise makers
- Prize for quiz show

Early arrivals.

Because all students don't arrive at the same time, it is important to prepare for those who do come early. As students arrive, ask each student to complete the **"Signs Page"** (instruction below) Instructions are to write under each sign what they think that sign represents. (To construct a **Signs Page** put together on a single piece of paper cutouts from publications that depict a variety of signs-stop signs, music signs, flags, etc.)

Gathering – 10 minutes.

To introduce the students to the importance of symbols in their lives, divide the group into pairs. Ask each pair to notice any symbols (clothes, jewelry, hair, shoes, etc.) on the other person. Gather group together and allow each person to share what symbols they noticed and then guess what they might mean to the other person.

Opening - 5 minutes.

Ask students to explain the meaning of the statement, *"Do Not Judge a Book by its Cover."* Accept all answers.

Share the reading of scripture from *Matthew 15: 10-11.* Ask if they see a connection between the scripture and the above statement.

> *"Listen and understand: it is not what goes into the mouth that defiles*
> *a man, but what comes out of the mouth, this defiles a man."*
> (Matt.15:10-11 RSV)

Ask the group to respond to above biblical statement:

Sanctuary scavenger hunt work sheet Take a walk with your eyes wide open through the sanctuary of your church.

Look carefully at the narthex, the foyer, the nave, the altar, and at the stained glass windows. Notice all the symbols present and write down those you particularly want your group to notice.

Try your hand at rough drawings of symbols you see. Go to *wwwfisheater.com/symbols* for help with drawings and meanings. Some symbols can be transferred electronically to your work sheet for the scavenger hunt.

Now get creative. Put together a scavenger hunt worksheet from your viewing of the symbols in your sanctuary. Pose questions or make statements to act as clues for the student's hunt for that symbol. Examples:

- Where can you find a fish, a cross, a butterfly?
- How many crosses are in the sanctuary?
- Find something you see after a rain storm when the sun comes out. (Rainbow)
- What symbols are at the ends of the pews?

Give each student a worksheet with the clues or questions and a time limit to locate the items in the sanctuary.

Responding - 10 minutes.

Discussion Time. Your purpose for the scavenger hunt is to excite curiosity. Now it's time to let the symbols teach faith formation to the students. Follow up with feedback about the meanings of the symbols. Some examples of symbols used for teaching include:

- Stained glass picture of Jesus as shepard – talk about the role of shepard as a caring figure.
- Trinity shield – Introduce the idea of a father in many roles (husband, father, son, worker,coach) but still one person. Introduce concept of God as Father, Son, and Holy Ghost, three in one.
- Empty cross – Convey concept of risen Christ (Easter).
- Communion table, Chalice – Focus conversation on the sacrament and the idea of connecting with Jesus.

Closing - 10 minutes.

Words are perhaps the most important symbols used by young people. What they say to or about each other become the basis for forming friendships or making enemies.

Reference: *"But what comes out of the mouth, this defiles a man.""*(Matthew 15: 11RSV)

Sit on floor in a circle. Leader suggests that each participant respond silently to the following guided meditation:

Take a deep breath and let it out slowly…(pause).

Now think of the last time you used a word or phrase intentionally meant to hurt another person (pause).

Remembering that words are symbols of how we feel and what we experience, how did those hurtful words make you feel? (pause).

If you could use words as a symbol of how you feel this very moment, what words would you use? (pause).

Open your eyes now. Look at the other people with whom you have shared this hour. They are a bundle of symbols. Each one was made in the image of God. Think about what that image looks like. Amen and Amen.

Alternative activities. The wedding ring symbol.

Gather the group in a half circle facing you. Fidget with your wedding ring (or borrow one) until it falls on the floor. Make a point of asking one of the students to pick it up for you and return it. Place it back on your finger.

Ask: "Do you know what this is?"

Most will reply: "Yes, it's a wedding ring."

Ask: "Do you know how much this is worth?"

Most will haunch their shoulders, but a few will take some wild guesses.

Respond: "I paid this much for it… (suggest a price $)." Probably much less than the group thinks it is worth.

Respond: "That's right. Wedding rings don't have to cost a lot, but they are very valuable. It's what it symbolizes that makes it valuable." Spend a few minutes discussing the symbolism of the wedding ring

The ring itself is merely a circle of semi-precious metal. The cost is not what's important. What it symbolizes is important. The ring points to a real experience; a commitment to another person. Its value as a symbol is far beyond its commercial value.

"Is it in our church or not?" – A symbols quiz show.

Draw up a list of Christian symbols, some of which are actually in your church sanctuary and some that are not. These test the group's perception of the symbols located in the sanctuary that they have seen numerous times but without recognition.

Divide the group into two teams Give each team captain a bell or whistle.

Instructions for playing the quiz show.

- Tell the groups that you will name a Christian symbol.
- The team must decide if that symbol is in their church sanctuary or not.
- The first team to ring their bell gets to answer.
- A correct answer earns two points for the team.
- An incorrect answer loses one point for the team.
- After a set time or when all the symbols have been named, count up the points (plus and minus).
- Give a prize (chewing gum, life savers) to the members of the winning team.

For more information.

Our Christian Symbols, by Friedrich Rest, Pilgrim Press, Cleveland, Ohio 1982.

Saints, Signs, and Symbols, by W. Ellwood Post, Morehouse Publishing 1974.

Dictionary of Symbols, by Carl G. Liungman, Merkur International KB, 1974.

Addendum 9

HOW IMPORTANT ARE SYMBOLS

(A student worksheet for use in the symbols activity)

Cindy Jackson had a dream for herself, a dream that perhaps many females share. Ever since she was a little girl she admired her Barbie Doll. She thought Barbie was the epitome of how every beautiful girl should look. She wanted to look beautiful too; long-limbed, big busted, small-waisted, with a pert nose, cute face, and long blonde hair.

Her Barbie Doll symbolized Cindy's dream of beauty. Barbie represented the famine ideal. Cindy Jackson, however, was just an average looking, plain girl from Ohio. But that didn't keep her from dreaming about Barbie's glamorous lifestyle.

As she grew toward adulthood, she inherited a small sum from a relative. This money allowed Cindy to think about her dream. Almost immediately she began to use her new found wealth for numerous plastic surgeries that would eventually transform her into a Barbie look-alike. So far, as much as we can tell, Cindy is happy with her new looks.

Barbie was a powerful symbol for Cindy Jackson, a symbol of her image of what she wanted to look like, and to a certain extent, to be like. It motivated her to action, to effectively change her life almost completely. She aspired to become the person the symbol of Barbie cultivated in her. Responding to symbols has the power to change a person forever. Cindy is not alone in her attempt to live out her dream.

Cindy's dream may be extreme; but teenagers and adults are like walking advertisements. We purchase tee shirts, hats, back packs embossed with Nike swoosh symbols, certain types of sneakers endorsed by Shak O'Neil, and images of our favorite heavy-metal bands or sports teams all in an effort to symbolize the kind of person or image we think we would like to be

Personal symbol quiz.

Underline the following "circumstances" that pertain to you:

I wear my hat backwards.

I only wear one brand of sneakers.

I choose friends by how popular they are.

I let my pants sag and my underwear show.

My cell phone is color-coordinated.

Cheer leaders are the most popular girls in school.

Being a nerd is…just nerdy.

When my parents drive me to school, I ask them to let me off one block before the school.

Being thin is very important.

Only sports jocks get the girls.

I always hug my friends.

Boys read *Seventeen Magazine.*

I never say "Whatever."

I'm not a member of a clique.

Prefer internet to TV.

<u>Now</u> …from the list that you underlined, decide what each symbolizes about you and your image of yourself.

What are symbols and what do they mean?

Symbols can be words or designs or articles that represent ideas, emotions, or experiences. The word dog is not a dog, but it reminds us of a dog. We associate the word dog with a particular dog or an experience we had with a dog. A four leaf clover is a symbol of good luck. The heart is a symbol of love.

There are other symbols that are easily recognizable. The American flag is a tangible representation of our country. We know that the flag isn't the country, but that it points to what our country stands for. The pledge of allegiance to the flag is not a statement of loyalty to a piece of fabric but of our loyalty to the experience of being an American. Symbols point to real things.

Symbols help people understand the important words someone is saying or writing. Symbols are different from pictures. The meaning of a picture may be unclear and mean different things to different people while a symbol focuses on a single concept. This means that symbols offer precise information.

Christian symbols.

Communicating our Christian faith depends heavily upon the use of symbols. Jesus often used simple things like coins and nets and sheep to communicate important concepts like integrity, salvation, and resurrection.

The sanctuaries of most churches are filled with Christian symbols. The Greek letters "alpha" and "omega," the first and last letters in their alphabet remind us that the bible says God is the first and the last. The butterfly is often used to symbolize the resurrection because the butterfly, like Christ, goes through a transformation (metamorphosis) from appearing to die to coming to life again in a different form.

The Christian symbols we use are not the Christian faith. We don't believe in or have faith in the symbols. Rather, the symbols "point" to a spiritual experience, a reality about God that we have experienced and do believe is the truth. The empty cross on the altar symbolizes the reality that Jesus was crucified on a cross but is no longer dead. Instead, we believe Jesus rose from the dead and we experience Jesus' presence as living among us.

Questions for consideration.

In the sacrament of Holy Communion, bread and wine are used as symbols. What do they symbolize? When you eat the bread and drink the cup that is also a symbolic action.

What does that symbolize?

What Christian symbols mean the most to you? What do they mean? Can you explain their meaning to another person? Do you think that other person understands?

Christian gangs.

> *Oregon: "Gang-related behavior" is the reason being given for two Albany teenagers who were suspended for wearing crucifixes, which they say were given to them by their mothers. Marco Castro, 16, and Jaime Salazar, 14, ignored orders to remove them.*
>
> *According to Salazar, Principal Chris Equinoa gave the order. Although not banned, he said he can still ask students to hide or remove items he feels have a connection to gangs. A local church said they've heard no reports of crucifixes used by gangs.*
>
> *Nearby towns say they have dealt with this for years, and say it could indicate their spread. Familiar with gangs, Equinoa used to work in Southern California schools, and said "We don't want to see it get to that point."*
>
> (Anonymous internet quote).

Your response.

- Do you think these students should not wear their crucifixes in school?
- Is being a Christian being part of a gang?
- How powerful is the symbol of a cross for you?
- What does the cross symbolize for you?

Christian pep rally.

More than 22,000 evangelical teenagers prayed, sang and screamed at AT&T Park today during BattleCry - a mix of pep rally, rock concert, and church service. *"We're all wrapped-up in Noah's Rainbow, as a symbol of God's promise to find new and exciting ways to kill us all next time. Drowning is so 2448 BC."* (SFGate.com, March 11, 2001).

- Does dressing yourself in a Christian symbol make you more faithful?

- What Christian symbols do you wear? Why?
- What Christian symbols are most important to you? What makes them important?
- Think about an important Christian symbol – the cross, the communion elements of bread and wine – describe how and why it is important to you.

Addendum 10

SPIRITUAL HEART ATTACKS

Luke 10: 38-42

(*First developed for adults, but found this theme valuable for teens. It encourages dialogue*)

Theme statement.

Resentments cause big problems. They get in the way of our relationships with others. They get in the way of our relationship with God. Jesus' insight into human relations allows him to resolve resentments, to heal hurting hearts, and in the process, open passageways to reconciliation with God.

Exploring the word.

The teachings of Jesus are not mere meaningless platitudes meant to console the anxious and placate the distressed. They are as much calls to action as they are tranquilizers for the soul. They are meant to inspire growth in faith, help reveal the mysteries of God and, more important, encourage us to consider consequences.

In this text, as with the surrounding texts, the consequences are what make the difference. Obedience to Jesus' teachings demand consequences, often in ways not expected. The life of a disciple is never easy.

Three incidences make up the latter part of Luke 10. At first glance they seem unrelated, but upon closer examination there is the common thread of "obedience" running through them. A lawyer asks Jesus, *"What must I do to inherit eternal life?"*(Vs. 25-28 RSV) to which the response is obedience – *"love God and love your neighbor."* Then comes the question of who is my neighbor (Vs. 29 RSV). In the Parable of the Good Samaritan, Jesus never answers the question of "who", but rather describes "how;" how obedience to God requires one to act toward a neighbor.

Finally, in our text for study, obedience takes on a new dimension. Jesus is welcomed into the house of Mary and Martha in keeping with his own directive *"Whenever you enter a town and its people welcome you, eat what is set before you"* (Vs. 8 RSV). But the response of Mary is unexpected and Martha's reaction to Jesus' acceptance of Mary is even more surprising. Despite Martha's objection to having to do all the work of the house hold while Mary sits at the feet of Jesus just listening, the mandate of Jesus is clear. *"Man does not live by bread alone, but by every word that comes from the mouth of God"* (Matthew 4:4 RSV). Obedience, in this context, refers to a devotion to the Lord's words as an expression of one's love for God.

The setting vs. 38. Jesus, along with some of his disciples, is on a journey traveling toward Jerusalem. It is a period during which the Pharisees confront Jesus with many questions about the Kingdom of God, his personal authority, and the meaning behind his many teachings. Keeping with his mandate to meet with the people who welcome him, he accepts the invitation of Martha to stay in her home. Martha appears to be the head of household as she is the one who assumes responsibility for the physical necessities that Jesus might require. Martha has a sister, Mary, who Jesus immediately recognizes as the more introspective of the two sisters.

The circumstances vs. 39. Mary, instead of helping her sister with the responsibilities of being a hostess, chooses to sit at the feet of Jesus enthralled, just listening and absorbing. The implication is that Mary usurps her social responsibilities setting herself up for disappointment from Martha.

Resentment emerges vs. 40. Martha expresses irritation at her sister's actions. More than embarrassed, she seems resentful. Martha's stilted perspective focuses mostly on herself and her life. *"Do you not care that my sister has left me to do all the work by myself?"*(RSV) She reacts to Jesus' attention to Mary by thinking it an insult to herself. *"Tell her then to help me."*(RSV) Her resentment is misplaced. Mary is the scapegoat for Martha's dissatisfaction with her own life. She is having a spiritual heart attack.

Healing begins vs. 41. Jesus, acting as spiritual physician, diagnoses many cases of spiritual heart disease. He recognizes Martha's festering resentment immediately. Just as resentment gets in the way of our relationships with each other, it also prevents us from a relationship with God. Jesus admonishes Martha for allowing worldly considerations to get in the way of hearing the word of God.

Resentment overcome vs. 42. Once again, Jesus' insight into human relations allows him to heal a hurting heart and in the process open a passageway toward reconciliation with God. Martha's resentment infects her soul like a poisonous fruit. *"There is need of only one thing,"* (RSV) Jesus reminds her. Focus on obedience and devotion to God.

The word today.

The heart is an amazing organ. Shaped a bit like a strawberry, only a little larger, it does the work of a powerful engine keeping the blood flowing day in and day out. But despite the voracity of the heart to work physically, what catches our attention the most is the heart's quality as the seat of our emotions.

Heart disease can be spiritual as well as physical. To suffer from a "hardened heart," the consequence of emotional resentment, causes us as much pain and grief as the worst diagnosis of occluded arties. Sometimes festering for years undetected, resentment can erupt suddenly and without warning.

The stronger the love, the greater the potential for resentment. Perhaps that is why the little girl who was very angry with her father for refusing to allow her to watch a certain television program before she finished her homework could write a note to him – *"Dear Dad, I hate you. Love, Rebecca."* This is what happened to Martha. Surely Martha loved her sister Mary and because she loved her greatly, she was capable of resenting her greatly.

Resentment is a strong barrier to spiritual formation. As we struggle with our person to person relationships, our relationship to God suffers as a consequence. We become a resentful person in general. We internalize resentment, a kind of addiction we can't shake.

Resentment is a human emotion. Consequently, as an obstacle to a relationship with God, it appears to have its roots in what happens to Martha. More precisely, Jesus reminds us that what causes resentment is not what happens, but how we respond to what happens. Martha experiences pain in her own life, but instead of attempting to change herself, she avoids the pain by blaming others – she resents. She resents her sister. She resents Jesus for not admonishing her sister. She resents having to do work that previously she found satisfying.

Martha fails. She does not allow God to be in charge. She usurps the priority of God with her own expectations. Her resentment shuts out the sunlight of the spirit. Here is the test for Martha. Can she rejoice when the truth prevails and Jesus is honored even though she doesn't receive her share of benefits or prominence?

To be a disciple of Jesus, to follow his mandates to love God with all ones heart, and be not swayed by the distractions of busyness requires that we focus our lives. It is not just *about Jesus,* but what *Jesus is about,* that matters. What Jesus is about is encouraging us to give our full devotion to the Word of God. A life committed to God is a life free of resentment.

Questions for discussion

Beginnings.

- Respond to the following: "Resentment seems to be caused by what happens. Actually it's caused by how you respond to what happens."
- "Forgiveness is the only way to dissolve resentment." Is this true? How do you know?

Exploring the word.

- Picture the scene. Martha emerges from the kitchen, leaning on her broom, tapping her feet and waiting for

Jesus to respond to her question. *"Jesus, doesn't it bother you?"* You're not Jesus, but how would you respond to Martha?

- Speculate: What was Martha's response when Jesus says to her, *"Mary has chosen what is best?"*
- How would you explain to Martha that *"Man shall not live by bread alone, but by every word that proceeds from the mouth of God."* (Matthew 4:4 RSV)

The word today: response.

"Why is it that people with fewer talents, who work less and struggle little, get ahead while I remain stuck?" Divide into groups of three. Ask each group to propose (1) a meaning for this statement and (2) a means for counseling the person who feels this way. Each group shares with the whole group.

Notice in the text that there are no religious words, no religious symbols, and no religious connotations. So…what does the story reveal about our relationship with God? What makes this story "religious?" (If time permits) As a group, rewrite the story using "religious" words.

Closing prayer.

Lord, if Jesus were to come into our homes, let us each know that whatever busyness we are engaged in can never be more important than hearing the Word as Jesus has taught us. Encourage us to allow devotion to God to be a priority in our lives. Only by focusing on Him will we achieve the true freedom you promise to all who are faithful to You. Amen.

Addendum 11

LOSING YOUR LIVELIHOOD - Teacher instructions

(This worksheet is for teacher's use with student's worksheet in addendum 11)

John 5: 1-9

Objectives for the session.

1. The students will understand that excuse-making is a barrier to faith formation.
2. The students will learn Jesus' attitudes about prohibitions against working on the Sabbath.
3. The students will be confronted by Jesus' teachings that healing is both physical and spiritual.

Session preparation.

Background texts. As leader for this session, it is best to read John 5:1-18. This allows you to know and understand how the event in the text for this session (John 5:1-9) is interpreted by the religious authorities of the day and how the entire experience leads to Jesus homily in the following section (vs. 19-47). For our study this session will only reflect on vs. 1-9. Knowing what follows these verses helps the leader to understand the events in today's text more completely.

Materials needed: Each student needs to read *"The Life of Brian"* excerpt (at end of session) and have access to the RSV Bible. It's best for each to have a bible, but the group can share one. Since dialogue is the discussion format, have the chairs arranged in a circle, if possible, so that participants address and see each other directly.

Leader awareness. After presentation of the text and its biblical background and interpretation, the discussion questions and exercises involve the participants in dialogue about the theme of the session – excuse making. This topic can be highly subjective. There may be times when the discussion borders on personal experience, an experience that might be too subjective for participants to engage in discussion openly. Respect personal space and do not force reluctant students into participating when you sense hesitation.

Opening the session (optional for early arrivals). Have available three by five cards, enough for each participant and pencils. As early students arrive, ask each one to write down as many excuses they can remember for why they didn't do one of the tasks their teachers/friend/parent/peer asked them to do. Before the session begins, collect the cards. Pass them out at random to participants to read at the start of the session. Late arrivals do not do this exercise, but benefit from hearing the excuses.

Leaders reflections. Consider your role as leader of the group study to be that of enabler. Your task is to guide the group toward discovery of the implications of the text for their own lives. You need not be an authority, only a fellow inquirer. Remember that not all people respond to rational stimuli. Some prefer visual or experiential. Be prepared for differering responses to the questions. Pray that your leadership guides students toward faithfulness.

Bible text overview.

The Gospel of John is unique among the four gospels. Unlike the first three narratives about the life and ministry of Jesus, John appears more intent upon examining the humanness of Jesus; that Jesus was indeed fully God, but also fully human. Consequently, there is considerably more dialogue and discourse interweaved among the exploits of Jesus. Jesus is engaged in conversation, sometimes a bit contentious, particularly with those who question his authority. In addition, John seems intent upon providing some theological reflection. Whenever and wherever Jesus' actions occur, there is often an explanation following that describes these actions in light of what they mean as a way of revealing the mystery of God.

The particular text from John 5:1-9 for this session is integrated with the remainder of chapter five. The themes presented in this chapter follow a typical pattern unique to John. First there is an event (Jesus' healing of the man at the well) followed by a confrontation with the religious authorities concerning his healing of the man on a Sabbath, a day when work was prohibited. The authorities take issue with Jesus, probably looking for evidence to convince themselves and others that his radical views are outside the religious expectations of the day. The remainder of the chapter carries some theological reflection focusing on the relationship between Jesus and God as well as the witnessing of Jesus to God. Together, this pattern follows the typical pattern of John in which an event is followed by a homily which serves to explain some characteristics of God and our response to God.

The setting (vs. 1-3). This incident takes place in the city of Jerusalem during one of the religious festivals. Which festival is unknown, but not significant to the narrative. Jerusalem is the present hot-bed of religious activism. It is a place where he knows his presence must be acknowledged if he is to relate his message to the greatest number, but also a place where there is considerable opposition to his claims. He meets a man carrying his "mat" who claims to have been at the healing pool for many years. The pool sits just outside the city gate (Sheep Gate) and apparently is known for its magical powers of healing. The place name is "Bethzatha" (Hebrew) or "Bethsaida. Of interest is verse 7. A man is waiting for when the *"water is stirred up"*, as if only then does the water contain its healing powers. Why Jesus is at the pool, we can only speculate.

The circumstances vs. 5-6. (There is no verse 4 in the RSV Bible). Thirty eight years represents a very long time to hold out hope for healing. The length of time is secondary to the circumstances of the man's encounter with Jesus. There is no indication that Jesus knew about the man beforehand or that he made "an appointment" with the man. It appears to be a chance encounter despite that the text says *"he knew he had been there a long time."* As both an expression of concern as well as marking the first step toward recovery, without hesitation, Jesus asks, *"Do you want to be made well?*

The confrontation (vs. 7). This verse provides background information about the man. It is not mere speculation that he is afraid to make changes in his life. He would rather make excuses. His response to Jesus' question *"Do you want to be healed?"* is neither a definitive yes or no, but rather a prolonged diatribe of excuse making. He appears to want to blame others for his own shortcomings. He is afraid to take some initiative for fear of failure. Like the leper in *"The Life of Brian"*(see dialogue at end of session) he has made his livelihood out of scapegoating. It is reasonable to suppose that Jesus recognizes this characteristic, but doesn't acknowledge it at the time.

The response (vs. 8-9). Jesus performs a healing miracle. Despite that the man registers a protest; that Jesus couldn't heal him since he has been trying himself for so many years, without success. But the tactics of Jesus are without conditions. No exceptions. No extenuating circumstances. No stipulations. Just do it. *"Stand up, take your mat and walk."* There is no acknowledgment that the man's faith made him well or that because he believed in the authority of Jesus as spokesman for God that Jesus could perform this miracle. Only afterward is the man impressed by the powers of Jesus. All the more reason to suggest that the narrative helps us to see that excuse-making is a barrier to faith, a hindrance not easily overcome by one's self without the help of Jesus as the Christ.

Follow-up (vs. 10-16). The second theme takes form in these verses. The healing of the man at the pool is the event that triggers growing opposition to Jesus by the religious authorities of the day. Although referred to as "Jews", the term refers more to whoever opposes Jesus, rather than to these people being only Jews. When accused by the authorities of breaking a Sabbath Law while walking with his mat, the man acknowledges that it was Jesus who did the work, hence it is he that is responsible for the miscarriage of religious law.

Questions for discussion.

Beginnings.

This question is intended to open the issue of excuse-making for the group. The kinds of circumstances most likely to generate excuses include but are not limited to

1. Protection from vulnerability.
2. Buying time to re-examine complicated and compromising situations (procrastinating).
3. Getting intrusive questioners off our backs.
4. Covering up our incompetence.
5. Avoiding responsibility.

The second exercise requires students to undertake a continuum. With consideration for avoiding embarrassment, the leader can ask willing participants to explain their choices.

Exploring the word.

Vs. 15 introduces the issue of questioning Jesus' actions on the Sabbath when "work" is prohibited. This question explores the many mandates of Jesus that loving and serving the neighbor under any circumstances is a response in faith to Christian teachings. Help the students see a difference between self-centeredness and other-centeredness as posited by Jesus. Loving action is not "work".

Making excuses appears to be part of the lifestyle for the man at the pool. Help students recognize that scapegoating, relinquishing responsibility, and procrastination are also an integral part of our faith responses when obedience is required to the mandates of God.

There are no right answers to this third question. Speculation however should be encouraged to focus on how insightful Jesus is, about how excuse making is seen as a barrier to faith formation, and about how the radical religious responses of Jesus in his time generated opposition as much as they do in our time.

The word today.

This first question is best approached as a group response. Use a blackboard, poster board, or one student as recorder and list the contributions of each member. Emphasize that you are looking for ways that we (the class) struggle with excuses when we consider how we respond (or don't respond) to the mandates of our faith. Examples might include dishonesty, procrastination, ignorance, deception, fraud, self-centeredness, untrustworthiness, and lying.

Again, on the other side of the poster board or blackboard or with a student recorder, construct a group listing of the resources that break down the excuse making barriers to faith formation. Examples might include honesty, self-responsibility, other centeredness, knowledge, trustworthiness, and obedience.

Closing.

Before concluding the session (optional) with prayer, ask students to complete the following sentence: "Excuse-making is a barrier to faith because…"

Prayer (to share with group).

Lord, so often are prayers to you are said with no expectation that you are listening. Sometimes we offer our own excuses, convincing ourselves that You are too busy to hear us. Help us to know that you hear our every thought, every word, and that we can pray expecting an answer. Amen.

The Life of Brian: (excerpt) by Monty Python *(Also available in student worksheet in Addendum 11 This section can be printed out separately for each student to read.)*

Ex-Leper: Okay, sir, my final offer: half a shekel for an old ex-leper?

Brian: Did you say "ex-leper"?

Ex-Leper: That's right, sir, 16 years behind a veil and proud of it, sir.

Brian: Well, what happened?

Ex-Leper: Oh, cured, sir.

Brian: Cured?

Ex-Leper: Yes sir, bloody miracle, sir. Bless you!

Brian: Who cured you?

Ex-Leper: Jesus did, sir. I was hopping along, minding my own business, all of a sudden, up he comes, cures me! One minute I'm a leper with a trade, next minute my livelihood's gone. Not so much as a by-your-leave! "You're cured, mate." Bloody do-gooder.

Addendum 12

LOSING YOUR LIVELIHOOD – Student

(Student worksheet to accompany teacher prep in addendum 10)

(Although originally devised for adult education, this session can be easily used by teenagers in confirmation.)

John 5:1-9

Theme statement.

Making excuses provides us with a certain amount of security. We grow use to them. We offer up excuses rather than take responsibility. But excuse-making in our relationship with God can become a major barrier to authentic faith. A study of this text reveals how Jesus challenges us to change from indecision to resolution as a prerequisite for faithfulness.

Exploring the word.

Two themes are present in this section of the text (John 5:1-18). The first occurs with Jesus' confrontation with the man at the pool. Jesus' action is as much a challenge to the man's inability to act as it is an example of Jesus' ability to perform healing miracles. Jesus heals the man, but more importantly he announces it to the religious authorities. This leads to the second theme. Jesus has violated a religious law that prohibits work on the Sabbath (day of rest). The premonition is that the "authorities" are out to find an excuse to kill Jesus. The first narrative (John 5:1-8) provides the evidence for the second (John 5:10-18). Because Jesus "worked" on the Sabbath, he is guilty of breaking the religious laws.

This study will focus on the first theme in which the text speaks of how Jesus confronts a man who is sick but unable to serve himself. Jesus suspects it is because of his excuse-making, his focus on scapegoating and blaming others for his own shortcomings.

The setting (vs. 1-3). Although the text gives no clues as to what festival is occurring, it does place Jesus in Jerusalem. Some differences occur in locating the pool and stating its name, but clearly it was a pool with apparent magical powers visited by invalids of all types just outside the city gate (Sheep Gate).

The circumstances (vs. 5-6, there is no vs. 4). No one knows for sure how long the man had been coming to the pool. Thirty-eight years is apparently a euphemism for the endurance of the man's circumstance. Jesus recognizes both his need for healing as well as his reluctance to self-start the process. There is little empathy on the part of Jesus, only a curt *"do you want to be healed?"* It is possible to interpret Jesus' response as his recognition that the man has grown used to being sick, has accepted it as a part of his life, and finds some security in his condition. Only Jesus' admonition will make a difference.

The confrontation (vs. 7). Unlike the people that Jesus meets, there seems to be no urgency with this man. One day is pretty much like all the others. Despite his mild protestations – *"Sir I have no one to put me into the pool…someone else steps up ahead of me"*- the man gives little indication that he really wants to change. He is comfortable with the excuses he provides. He blames others for his lack of initiative. This is an indication that he doesn't want to change his livelihood, certainly not with any intense compulsion.

The response (vs. 8-9). Jesus immediately recognizes that this man is a compulsive excuse–maker; blaming other people for circumstances he claims are beyond his control. Without empathy, but with regard for human sanctity, Jesus immediately heals him with a command, *"Stand up, take your mat and walk."* Uncharacteristically, Jesus does not acknowledge, as he does in other narratives, that the man's faith has made him well. It's almost as if the man irritates Jesus with his excuses, but takes pity on him, recognizing that he will only continue to sit there and make excuses for another thirty-eight years, so he might as well heal him and be done with it.

Follow up (vs. 10-16). Although not part of our study text for this session, the following verses complete the theme of this narrative. When questioned by the authorities about walking with his mat, apparently a violation of the rule of not working on the Sabbath, the man confesses that it was Jesus who healed him (another excuse by blaming someone beside himself). Thus, the stage is set for the authorities to confront Jesus with breaking the Sabbath rules.

The word today.

In the Monty Python movie, *The Life of Brian,* (1979) there is a scene in act 56 where Brian is accosted by a group of beggars. The dialogue and action that follow go something like this: (Students should have this selection to read individually).

In a solicitous tone, the first beggar calls out, "Okay sir, my final offer" half a shekel; for an old ex-beggar."

"Did you say, ex-beggar?" Brian asks.

"That's right, sir. 16 years behind a veil and proud of it, sir."

"Well what happened?" Brian asks him.

"Oh, cured, sir."

"Cured?" Brian asks

"Yes sir, bloody miracle, sir. Bless you."

"Who cured you?" asks Brian.

"Jesus did sir. I was hopping along, minding my own business, all of a sudden, up he comes, cures me. One minute I'm a leper with a trade, next minute my livelihood's gone."

I can't be positive, but it sure sounds as if this scene was taken directly from the Gospel of John (John 5: 1-9). The characters change and the scene differs slightly, but the excuse is the same. We get the distinct impression that this man (ex-leper) was quite comfortable with his affliction, but hesitant to admit it. He has grown comfortable with his excuses. They offer him a sense of security. *"Please don't make me give them up. I've gotten used to them. I know how to be a leper. Without my leprosy I feel as vulnerable as a new born baby."*

Excuse-making can, and does, serve other purposes besides that of just avoiding responsibility. We turn to excuses for lots of reasons:

- Excuses protect us when we feel vulnerable.
- Excuses buy extra time to solve a problem.
- Excuses get intrusive questioners off our backs.

Excuse-making is a major barrier to the formation of an authentic faith. The relationship we foster with God is often fraught with excuses. *"But they all alike began to make excuses"* (Luke 14:18 RSV). We harbor excuses out of self-centeredness, fears of rejection, and false concepts of reality. *"If I had not come and spoken to them, they would not have sin, but now they have no excuse for their sin."* (John 15: 22 RSV).

Despite yearning to be in right relationship with God, we contend that it is not possible. Jesus declares that as an excuse. That is why the question posed by Jesus, *"Do you want to be healed?"*(vs. 6) is so revealing. Like the man at the pool, we have never thought to ask ourselves this question and we are unprepared to answer. Whatever kept the man glued to his static position is probably the same dynamic that keeps us immobile and whining and blaming – the fear of being hurt or rejected, the fear of looking foolish, and the fear of not being acceptable in the eyes of God.

From God's perspective, we learn there is only one sin – chosen separation from God. Each time we choose to separate ourselves from God, we have an excuse for so doing. And yet the text is telling us that Jesus can heal, can connect us with God, and can set us in right relationship with God, but only if we want.

Questions for discussion.

Beginnings.

- "The dog ate my homework." Under what kinds of circumstances are you most likely to offer an excuse?

- What do you fear most as your reason for excuse-making? (Place 1 under the greatest fear and 4 under least fear

Rejection	Being unprepared	Being exposed	Your self-centeredness

Exploring the word.

- As a result of healing the man at the pool, Jesus is criticized for working on the Sabbath (John 5:15). How do you distinguish between sacred work and secular work?
- What do you suppose was the "real ailment" of the man at the pool?
- Speculate. What does this passage tell you about Jesus? About his ministry? About opposition to Jesus?

The word today.

- As a group task, formulate a listing of excuses that appear to be barriers to practicing (or following) your faith as you would want to.
- Again, as a group, formulate a list of resources that can enable you to take full responsibility for your talk and actions. Think about both secular and religious resources and the connection between the two.

Closing prayer.

Lord, so often our prayers to You are said with no expectation that You are listening. Sometimes we offer our own excuses, convincing ourselves that You are too busy to hear us. Help us to know that You hear our every thought, every word, and that we can pray expecting an answer. Amen.

Addendum 13

SIMPLE ACTIVITIES TO ENHANCE CONFIRMATION EDUCATION

Each of the following activates can be used to encourage dialogue and discussion with teenagers. Dialogue serves to enhance their ability to think creedal; to articulate about their Christian faith. Use these at will with any of the chapters or addendums

1.Knowledge of the Bible

Gathering time (5-15 minutes).

"Are You Smarter Than a Fifth Grade Sunday School Student?"

Preparations.

Prepare a poster board with categories listed but not the questions.

Christian Holidays: (questions – Easter comes on a different date each year, or Pentecost begins how many days after Easter?)

It's In the Bible: (questions – Moses was born in what country? Who was the father of Isaac?)

Christian History: (questions – The (denomination) was founded by whom? How old is our local church?)

Famous Bible Stories: (questions – How many brothers did the prodigal son have? Who was swallowed by a whale?)

Things I Should Have Known If I Were Paying Attention In Sunday school? questions –(Why do we call this church a "Lutheran" church?" The trinity means God in _______ persons?)

Divide the group into two teams. Each person gets to answer one question in one category. Two points if answer is correct. One point if team members are consulted. Continue until all categories and questions are used. (You can substitute other questions of your choice in the categories or add categories).

2. *It's In the bible, or not.* A quiz show game

Preparations.

- A bell or whistle for each team
- A list of "Saying of Jesus", some in the bible and some made up (see "Sayings Of Jesus " below.)

Instruction for playing.

- Divide group into two teams
- Give each time a "noise maker" (bell or whistle).
- Read from the list of "sayings of Jesus:" and ask, "Is it in the Bible, or Not?"
- First team to ring bell gets to answer
- If answer is correct they get two points. If answer is incorrect they lose one point.
- Continue play until all "sayings have been shared or time runs out.

Potential "sayings of Jesus". (yes means in the bible, no means not in the bible

God helps those who help themselves – NO.
God in three person, Blessed trinity – NO.
Blessed are the poor in spirit – YES.
Blessed are the meek – YES.
You are the salt of the earth – YES.
God is like salt for he pours his goodness on everyone – NO.
Let the oppressed go free – YES.
Forgive those who love you as God has forgiven you – NO.
The pen is mightier than the sword – NO.

Stand up and walk – YES.
Take your bed and go to your home – YES.
I do strange things that you won't believe – NO.
Blessed are the tax collectors – NO.
Blessed is the bread of life that I give you – NO.
He has anointed me to bring good news to the poor – YES.
He has anointed me to spare the children from sin – NO.
He sent me to bring recovery of sound to the deaf – NO.

3.Bible demonstrations.

Divide into groups of three. Have two people carry the third a short distance to demonstrate the difficulty of being a paraplegic.

(Blowing the air horn is a method to get immediate attention)

Blow air horn or clap hands. (Don't shout) Give each student a piece of bread. Have them butter the bread from 1. Unsalted butter, and 2. Salted butter. Ask students to guess which butter had the salt, demonstrating the statement of Jesus *"If salt has lost its taste how can it be restored"*?

Blow air horn and shout "time out". In teams of two, blindfold one student and have the other catch blinded student when they fall backwards to demonstrate how important trust and sight is. (Jesus recovery of sight to the blind – Luke 4)

Blow air horn. (Don't shout). Have prepared some insults about being a teenager on poster board (Stupid, followers, gangly, uncoordinated, ignorant, etc.) Accuse them of these descriptions and ask how that made them feel. Demonstrate that Jesus came to comfort and change the lives of those who were persecuted.

4.Guided Meditations

Participate in a guided meditation based on content of Sermon on the Mount (Matthew 5) and Jesus' rejection at Nazareth (Luke 4). Ask students to respond silently to each section of the meditation as you read:

Close your eyes and take a deep breath...Let it out slowly... (pause).

Jesus says those who are poor will be blessed. Think about what causes poverty. Now think about how you can help eliminate it... pause).

*Jesus says those who seek peace should be blessed. Where is peace needed in our world?...*pause).

Jesus says he comes to release captives and the oppressed. Pray silently for those you know who might be captives or oppressed... (pause).

Open your eyes ... Take another long, deep breath...(pause) Amen and Amen.

5. My faith story. Sermon on the Mount.

The focus of these texts is about the power of God working through Jesus to bring change to people in need. It implies that we glorify God by how we honor each other. Bring news stories that reflect human service. Share experiences you have had of faith at work. Describe your mission experiences and why you chose to participate. How does mission and outreach reflect expectations of God or human faithfulness? What risks does the person take that chooses to help others?

Guest speakers.

"Faith Without Works Is Dead"

Gather a group of adults who have participated in mission projects. Ask them to respond to *"So faith by itself, if it has no works, is dead."* (James 2: 17). Encourage them to use simple language and illustrations with which youth can connect. Contact a local Salvation Army Service Unit and arrange for a "Salvationist" or volunteer to describe the mission of the Salvation Army.

Bible connection, hope for the hopeless.

Use the text from Luke 4:18-19 as the teaching tool. Tell students that what Jesus says is not new, but is rather his understanding of fulfilling the message of the Old Testament (Isaiah 58: 6 and 61: 1-2). Break down the text into tasks:

- Bring good news to the poor
- Proclaim release to the captives
- Recovery of sight to the blind
- Letting the oppressed go free

Divide students into four groups. Instruct each group to corroborate on determining who are the poor, the captives, the blind, and the oppressed. Share findings of small groups with large group.

On poster board, write a different phrase at the top of seven columns: "1.*poor in spirit,* 2. *those who mourn,* 3.*the meek,* 4.*those who hunger,* 5.*the merciful,* 6.*the pure in heart,* and 7.*the peacemakers*. Students who have participated in mission trips may be able to find connections between people they observed in the field and the mandates of Jesus in the bible.

One by one, ask each student to come forward to write under one column a circumstance they have witnessed that describes a person in that column.

Bring in a doctor's prescription pad. Share with students that when they are sick, the doctor considers what medication might be best to relieve their symptoms and make them better. Give each student a blank prescription sheet. Ask them to read Luke 4:18-19, decide on one of the maladies, and write a prescription that will best relieve the malady. *Share the prescriptions with the whole group.*

Jesus is chastised by the authorities for healing a sick person (Luke 5: 20-26). Tape a Sunday morning TV evangelists (i.e. Benny Hinn, Slalmat Khokhar, Joel Osteen) and show portions to class. Ask opinion of group about the faith healing experience.

Science connection. Appearances can be misleading.

Materials needed. Give a clear marble to each student. Provide some small pictures or objects that will be visible when looking at them through the marble. Be sure that the light in your experiment area is sufficient.

Experiment. Ask each student to focus on a picture or object while looking through the marble. The image of whatever they are looking at will appear upside down.

Use this to introduce that appearances can be misleading. Refer to Jesus' use of "appearances" in the Sermon on the Mount; that the meek will prevail, those who mourn will be comforted, the poor in spirit will enter the Kingdom, and the hungry will be replenished

Discussion.

- What are some ways Jesus turns our world upside down?
- Describe a time you felt "turned around"
- How is looking through the marble the same as looking through "faithful eyes"?
- How does our faith affect how we view the world?

(Adapted from suggestion by Dave Mahoney, Fairfield Church of Christ, Lancaster, Ohio)

6.The Mysteries of God

Object lesson. What makes it work

Materials. Gather a variety of electrical and electronic objects – cell phone, camera, game boy, iPod, and/or calculator.

Activity. Ask students to describe how each works. Make questions difficult to demonstrate that they really don't know the particulars or details. Remind the students that just because we don't know all the details about why something works don't mean we can't benefit from it. Example: we use a computer to solve problems but may not know details of how it works. We drive cars without knowing details of internal combustion engine.

Application. We may have many unanswered questions about the mystery of God but that doesn't mean that we can't trust God. Jesus does an amazing amount of healing without our understanding how, but we can still trust that he possess the power of God.

If Jesus claims that with faith in him the oppressed will be freed, the captives will be released, the blind will see and the poor will be justified, just because we don't understand the "how," we can still trust that it will be so. (The above is adapted from CreativeYouthIdeas.Com)

7.Your Sins are Forgiven – Helping others

Learning in motion. Friends helping friends

Materials. Write out scenarios for pairs of students in which someone would need help. Examples:

- An untied shoe.
- Each person has one hand only.
- Help partner tie shoe.

Or

- Your partner can't walk.
- Help partner across room.

Or

- Partner lies limp on floor.
- Other partner must undress his shirt.

Fold up scenarios and put in basket. Pair off in groups of two. Each pair picks a scenario from the basket and acts out the situation. Ask for response to the difficulty in helping others.

Closing time.

- Do you think there is any connection between human behavior and physical; sickness. Jesus says "which is easier to say, your sins are forgiven you, or to say stand up and walk." What do you think he was talking about?
- How will you know when the "spirit of the Lord" is upon you?
- Why do you feel Jesus is so intent upon expressing his thoughts in roundabout, upside down fashion?"

Closing ritual.

Pre-record and play the song by the U2"s *I Still Haven't Found What I'm Looking For"* (The Joshua Tree, 1987) Pass out pencils and 3x5 cards with the sentence, "One way I live that Jesus encourages is…"(open ended) written on them." Read to the group Luke 4:18-19. Ask each person to complete the sentence on the 3x5 card (three minutes). Close the session by asking for volunteers to share what they have written.

Closing blessing.

May you live your life not afraid of what others think. My you continue to serve others even if they don't serve you. Be a friend to the friendless and give hope to the hopeless. Know that Jesus will be with you all the way. Amen and amen.

Note. All of the above activities were derived from on line sources that are public domain. They are presented on line as resources to be used by teachers and pastors of teenagers.

www.ingramcontent.com/pod-product-compliance
Lightning Source LLC
Chambersburg PA
CBHW071429090426
42737CB00011B/1613
9781603500678